P9-DEU-990

TOPDOG/ UNDERDOG

BY SUZAN-LORI PARKS

DRAMATISTS
PLAY SERVICE
INC.

4 Paul Oscher
   who taught me how 2 throw the cards

INTRODUCTION

In January 1999 I was thinking about a play I'd written seven years earlier called *The America Play*. In that play's first act we watch a black man who has fashioned a career for himself: he sits in an arcade impersonating Abraham Lincoln and lets people come and play at shooting him dead — like John Wilkes Booth shot our sixteenth president in 1865 during a performance at Ford's Theatre. So I was thinking about my old play when another black Lincoln impersonator, unrelated to the first guy, came to mind: a new character for a new play. This time I would just focus on his home life. This new Lincoln impersonator's real name would be Lincoln. He would be a former 3-card monte hustler. He would live with his brother, a man named Booth.

My interest in 3-card monte began one day when my husband, Paul, and I were walking along Canal Street and saw some guys doing the shell game. I was fascinated because, while I'd seen the scam before, this time I had someone whispering a running commentary in my ear, a kind of play-by-play, explaining the ins and outs of the scam, what was really going down. Sure enough the commentator was my husband. Turns out that, back in the days when he played in the Muddy Waters Blues Band, Paul would, for fun, hustle 3-card monte between sets. So when we got home that day he sat me down and showed me how to throw the cards.

This is a play about family wounds and healing. Welcome to the family.

Suzan-Lori Parks
April 2002

AUTHOR'S NOTE

From my "Elements of Style" —

I'm continuing the use of my slightly unconventional theatrical elements. Here's a road map.

(Rest)
Take a little time, a pause, a breather; make a transition.

A Spell
An elongated and heightened *(Rest)*. Denoted by repetition of characters' names with no dialogue. Has sort of an architectural look:
LINCOLN.
BOOTH.
LINCOLN.
BOOTH.
This is a place where the characters experience their pure true simple state. While no action or stage business is necessary, directors should fill this moment as they best see fit.

(Parentheses around dialogue indicate softly spoken passages (asides; sotto voce)).

Brackets, [ ], indicate possible cuts for production.

TOPDOG/UNDERDOG opened at the Joseph Papp Public Theater/New York Shakespeare Festival (George C. Wolfe, Producer; Fran Reiter, Executive Director; Rosemarie Tichler, Artistic Director) in New York City on July 26, 2001. It was directed by George C. Wolfe; the set design was by Riccardo Hernandez; the lighting design was by Scott Zielinski, the sound design was by Dan Moses Schreier; and the costume design was by Emilio Sosa. The cast was as follows:

LINCOLN .... Jeffrey Wright
BOOTH .... Don Cheadle

TOPDOG/UNDERDOG opened on Broadway at the Ambassador Theatre on April 7, 2002. It was directed by George C. Wolfe; the set design was by Riccardo Hernández; the costume design was by Emilio Sosa; the lighting design was by Scott Zielinski; the sound design was by Dan Moses Schreier; the production stage manager was Rick Steiger; and the stage manager was Gwendolyn M. Gilliam. The cast was as follows:

LINCOLN .... Jeffrey Wright
BOOTH .... Mos Def

THE PLAYERS

LINCOLN, the topdog

BOOTH (aka 3-Card), the underdog

PLACE

Here.

TIME

Now.

I am God in nature;
I am a weed by the wall.

—Ralph Waldo Emerson
   From "Circles"
   Essays: First Series (1841)

TOPDOG/UNDERDOG

Scene One

*Thursday evening. A seedily furnished rooming house room.
A bed, a reclining chair, a small wooden chair, some other
stuff but not much else. Booth, a black man in his early
30s, practices his 3-card monte scam on the classic setup: 3
playing cards and the cardboard playing board atop 2 mis-
matched milk crates. His moves and accompanying patter
are, for the most part, studied and awkward.*

BOOTH.
Watch me close watch me close now: who-see-thuh-red-card-
who-see-thuh-red-card? I-see-thuh-red-card. Thuh-red-card-is-
thuh-winner. Pick-thuh-red-card-you-pick-uh-winner. Pick-uh-
black-card-you-pick-uh-loser. Theres-thuh-loser, yeah, theres-
thuh-black-card, theres-thuh-other-loser-and-theres-thuh-red-
card, thuh-winner.
(Rest)
Watch me close watch me close now: 3-Card-throws-thuh-cards-light-
ning-fast. 3-Card-thats-me-and-Ima-last. Watch-me-throw-cause-
here-I-go. One-good-pickll get-you-in, 2-good-picks-and-you-gone-
win. See-thuh-red-card-see-thuh-red-card-who-see-thuh-red-card?
(Rest)
Dont touch my cards, man, just point to thuh one you want. You-
pick-that-card-you-pick-a-loser, yeah, that-cards-a-loser. You-pick-
that-card-thats-thuh-other-loser. You-pick-that-card-you-pick-a-
winner. Follow that card. You gotta chase that card. You-pick-
thuh-dark-deuce-thats-a-loser-other-dark-deuces-thuh-other-

loser, red-deuce, thuh-deuce-of-heartsll-win-it-all. Follow thuh red card.

(Rest)

Ima show you thuh cards: 2 black cards but only one heart. Now watch me now. Who-sees-thuh-red-card-who-knows-where-its-at? Go on, man, point to thuh card. Put yr money down cause you aint no clown. No? Ah you had thuh card, but you didnt have thuh heart.

(Rest)

You wanna bet? 500 dollars? Shoot. You musta been watching 3-Card real close. Ok. Lay the cash in my hand cause 3-Cards thuh man. Thank you, mister. This card you say?

(Rest)

Wrong! Sucker! Fool! Asshole! Bastard! I bet yr daddy heard how stupid you was and drank himself to death just cause he didnt wanna have nothing to do witchu! I bet yr mama seen you when you was born and she wished she was dead, sucker! Ha Ha Ha! And 3-Card, once again, wins all thuh money!!

(Rest)

What? Cops looking my way? Fold up thuh game, and walk away. Sneak outa sight. Set up on another corner.

(Rest)

Yeah.

(Rest)

(Having won the imaginary loot and dodged the imaginary cops, Booth sets up his equipment and starts practicing his scam all over again. Lincoln comes in quietly. He is a black man in his later 30s. He is dressed in an antique frock coat and wears a top hat and fake beard, that is, he is dressed to look like Abraham Lincoln. He surreptitiously walks into the room to stand right behind Booth, who, engrossed in his cards, does not notice Lincoln right away.)

BOOTH.
Watch me close watch me close now: who-see-thuh-red-card-who-see-thuh-red-card? I-see-thuh-red-card. Thuh-red-card-is-thuh-winner. Pick-thuh-red-card-you-pick-uh-winner. Pick-uh-black-card-you-pick-uh-loser. Theres-thuh-loser-yeah-theres-thuh-

black-card, theres-thuh-other-loser-and-theres-thuh-red-card, thuh-winner. Don't touch my cards, man, don't —
(Rest)
Dont do that shit. Dont do that shit. Dont do that shit!

(Booth, sensing someone behind him, whirls around, pulling a gun from his pants. While the presence of Lincoln doesnt surprise him, the Lincoln costume does.)

BOOTH.
And woah, man dont *ever* be doing that shit! Who thuh fuck you think you is coming in my shit all spooked out and shit. You pull that one more time I'll shoot you!

LINCOLN.
I only had a minute to make the bus.

BOOTH.
Bullshit.

LINCOLN.
Not completely. I mean, its either bull or shit, but not a complete lie so it aint bullshit, right?
(Rest)
Put yr gun away.

BOOTH.
Take off the damn hat at least.

(Lincoln takes off the stovepipe hat. Booth puts his gun away.)

LINCOLN.
Its cold out there. This thing kept my head warm.

BOOTH.
I dont like you wearing that bullshit, that shit that bull that disguise that getup that motherdisfuckinguise anywhere in the daddy-dick-sticking vicinity of my humble abode.

(Lincoln takes off the beard.)

LINCOLN.
Better?

BOOTH.
Take off the damn coat too. Damn, man. Bad enough you got to wear that shit all day you come up in here wearing it. What my women gonna say?

LINCOLN.
What women?

BOOTH.
I got a date with Grace tomorrow. Shes in love with me again but she dont know it yet. Aint no man can love her the way I can. She sees you in that getup its gonna reflect bad on me. She coulda seen you coming down the street. Shit. Could be standing outside right now taking her ring off and throwing it on the sidewalk.

(Booth takes a peek out the window.)

BOOTH.
I got her this ring today. Diamond. Well, diamond-esque, but it looks just as good as the real thing. Asked her what size she wore. She say 7 so I go boost a size 6 and a half, right? Show it to her and she loves it and I shove it on her finger and its a tight fit right, so she cant just take it off on a whim, like she did the last one I gave her. Smooth, right?

(Booth takes another peek out the window.)

LINCOLN.
She out there?

BOOTH.
Nope. Coast is clear.

LINCOLN.
You boosted a ring?

BOOTH.
Yeah. I thought about spending my inheritance on it but — take off that damn coat, man, you make me nervous standing there looking like a spook, and that damn face paint, take it off. You should take all of it off at work and leave it there.

LINCOLN.
I dont bring it home someone might steal it.

BOOTH.
At least *take it off* there, then.

LINCOLN.
Yeah.
(Rest)

(Lincoln takes off the frock coat and applies cold cream, removing the whiteface.)

LINCOLN.
I was riding the bus. Really I only had a minute to make my bus and I was sitting in the arcade thinking, should I change into my street clothes or should I make the bus? Nobody was in there today anyway. Middle of the week middle of winter. Not like on weekends. Weekends the place is packed. So Im riding the bus home. And this kid asked me for my autograph. I pretended I didnt hear him at first. I'd had a long day. But he kept asking. Theyd just done Lincoln in history class and he knew all about him, he'd been to the arcade but, I dunno, for some reason he was tripping cause there was Honest Abe right beside him on the bus. I wanted to tell him to go fuck hisself. But then I got a look at him. A little rich kid. Born on easy street, you know the type. So I waited until I could tell he really wanted it, the autograph, and I told him he could have it for 10 bucks. I was gonna say 5, cause of the Lincoln connection but something in me made me ask for 10.

BOOTH.
But he didnt have a 10. All he had was a penny. So you took the penny.

LINCOLN.
All he had was a *20*. So I took the 20 and told him to meet me on the bus tomorrow and Honest Abe would bring him his change.

BOOTH.
Shit.

LINCOLN.
Shit is right.
(Rest)

BOOTH.
Whatd you do with thuh 20?

LINCOLN.
Bought drinks at Luckys. A round for everybody. They got a kick out of the getup.

BOOTH.
You shoulda called me down.

LINCOLN.
Next time, bro.
(Rest)
You making bookshelves? With the milk crates, you making book-shelves?

BOOTH.
Yeah, big bro, Im making bookshelves.

LINCOLN.
Whats the cardboard part for?

BOOTH.
Versatility.

LINCOLN.
Oh.

BOOTH.
I was thinking we dont got no bookshelves we dont got no dining room table so Im making a sorta modular unit you put the books in the bottom and the table top on top. We can eat and store our books. We could put the photo album in there.

(Booth gets the raggedy family photo album and puts it in the milk crate.)

BOOTH.
Youd sit there, I'd sit on the edge of the bed. Gathered around the dinner table. Like old times.

LINCOLN.
We just gotta get some books but thats great, Booth, thats real great.

BOOTH.
Dont be calling me Booth no more, K?

LINCOLN.
You changing yr name?

BOOTH.
Maybe.

LINCOLN.
BOOTH.

LINCOLN.
What to?

BOOTH.
Im not ready to reveal it yet.

LINCOLN.
You already decided on something?

BOOTH.
Maybe.

LINCOLN.
You gonna call yrself something african? That be cool. Only pick something thats easy to spell and pronounce, man, cause you know, some of them african names, I mean, ok, Im down with the power to the people thing, but, no ones gonna hire you if they cant say yr name. And some of them fellas who got they african names, no one can say they names and they cant say they names neither. I mean, you dont want yr new handle to obstruct yr employment possibilities.

BOOTH.
LINCOLN.

BOOTH.
You bring dinner?

LINCOLN.
"Shango" would be a good name. The name of the thunder god. If you aint decided already Im just throwing it in the pot. I brought chinese.

BOOTH.
Lets try the table out.

LINCOLN.
Cool.

(They both sit at the new table. The food is far away near the door.)

LINCOLN.
BOOTH.

LINCOLN.
I buy it you set it up. Thats the deal. Thats the deal, right?

BOOTH.
You like this place?

LINCOLN.
Ssallright.

BOOTH.
But a little cramped sometimes, right?

LINCOLN.
You dont hear me complain. Although that recliner sometimes Booth, man — no Booth, right — man, Im too old to be sleeping in that chair.

BOOTH.
Its my place. You dont got a place. Cookie, she threw you out. And you cant seem to get another woman. Yr lucky I let you stay.

LINCOLN.
Every Friday you say *mi casa es su casa.*

BOOTH.
Every Friday you come home with yr paycheck. Today is Thursday and I tell you brother, its a long way from Friday to Friday. All kinds of things can happen. All kinds of bad feelings can surface and erupt while yr little brother waits for you to bring in yr share.
(Rest)
I got my Thursday head on, Link. Go get the food.

(Lincoln doesnt budge.)

LINCOLN.
You dont got no running water in here, man.

19

BOOTH.
So?

LINCOLN.
You dont got no toilet you dont got no sink.

BOOTH.
Bathrooms down the hall.

LINCOLN.
You living in thuh Third World, fool! Hey, I'll get thuh food.

(Lincoln goes to get the food. He sees a stray card on the floor and examines it without touching it. He brings the food over, putting it nicely on the table.)

LINCOLN.
You been playing cards?

BOOTH.
Yeah.

LINCOLN.
Solitaire?

BOOTH.
Thats right. Im getting pretty good at it.

LINCOLN.
Thats soup and thats sauce. I got you the meat and I got me the skrimps.

BOOTH.
I wanted the skrimps.

LINCOLN.
You said you wanted the meat. This morning when I left you said you wanted the meat.

(Rest)
Here man, take the skrimps. No sweat.

(They eat. Chinese food from styrofoam containers, cans of soda, fortune cookies. Lincoln eats slowly and carefully, Booth eats ravenously.)

LINCOLN.
Yr getting good at solitaire?

BOOTH.
Yeah. How about we play a hand after eating?

LINCOLN.
Solitaire?

BOOTH.
Poker or rummy or something.

LINCOLN.
You know I dont touch thuh cards, man.

BOOTH.
Just for fun.

LINCOLN.
I dont touch thuh cards.

BOOTH.
How about for money?

LINCOLN.
You dont got no money. All the money you got I bring in here.

BOOTH.
I got my inheritance.

LINCOLN.
Thats like saying you dont got no money cause you aint never

21

gonna do nothing with it so its like you dont got it.

BOOTH.
At least I still got mines. You blew yrs.

LINCOLN.
BOOTH.

LINCOLN.
You like the skrimps?

BOOTH.
Ssallright.

LINCOLN.
Whats yr fortune?

BOOTH.
"Waste not want not." Whats yrs?

LINCOLN.
"Your luck will change!"

(Booth finishes eating. He turns his back to Lincoln and fiddles around with the cards, keeping them on the bed, just out of Lincolns sight. He mutters the 3-card patter under his breath. His moves are still clumsy. Every once and a while he darts a look over at Lincoln who does his best to ignore Booth.)

BOOTH.
((((Watch me close watch me close now: who-see-thuh-red-card-who-see-thuh-red-card? I-see-thuh-red-card. Thuh-red-card-is-thuh-winner. Pick-thuh-red-card-you-pick-uh-winner. Pick-uh-black-card-and-you-pick-uh-loser. Theres-thuh-loser, yeah, theres-thuh-black-card, theres-thuh-other-loser-and-theres-thuh-red-card, thuh-winner! Cop C, Stick, Cop C! Go on —))))

LINCOLN.
((Shit.))

BOOTH.
(((((((One-good-pickll-get-you-in, 2-good-picks-and-you-gone-win. Dont touch my cards, man, just point to thuh one you want. You-pick-that-card-you-pick-uh-loser, yeah, that-cards-uh-loser. You-pick-that-card-thats-thuh-other-loser. You-pick-that-card-you-pick-uh-winner. Follow-that-card. You-gotta-chase-that-card!)))))))

LINCOLN.
You wanna hustle 3-card monte, you gotta do it right, you gotta break it down. Practice it in smaller bits. Yr trying to do the whole thing at once thats why you keep fucking it up.

BOOTH.
Show me.

LINCOLN.
No. Im just saying you wanna do it you gotta do it right and if you gonna do it right you gotta work on it in smaller bits, thatsall.

BOOTH.
You and me could team up and do it together. We'd clean up, Link.

LINCOLN.
I'll clean up — bro.

(Lincoln cleans up. As he clears the food, Booth goes back to using the "table" for its original purpose.)

BOOTH.
My new names 3-Card. 3-Card, got it? You wanted to know it so now you know it. 3-card monte by 3-Card. Call me 3-Card from here on out.

LINCOLN.
"3-Card." Shit.

BOOTH.
Im getting everybody to call me 3-Card. Grace likes 3-Card better than Booth. She says 3-Cards got something to it. Anybody not calling me 3-Card gets a bullet.

LINCOLN.
Yr too much, man.

BOOTH.
Im making a point.

LINCOLN.
Point made, 3-Card. Point made.

(Lincoln picks up his guitar. Plays at it.)

BOOTH.
Oh, come on, man, we could make money you and me. Throwing down the cards. 3-Card and Link: look out! We could clean up you and me. You would throw the cards and I'd be yr Stickman. The one in the crowd who looks like just an innocent passerby, who looks like just another player, like just another customer, but who gots intimate connections with you, the Dealer, the one throwing the cards, the main man. I'd be the one who brings in the crowd, I'd be the one who makes them want to put they money down, you do yr moves and I do mines. You turn yr head and I turn the card —

LINCOLN.
It aint as easy as all that. Theres —

BOOTH.
We could be a team, man. Rake in the money! Sure thered be some cats out there with fast eyes, some brothers and sisters who would watch real close and pick the right card, and so thered be some days when we would lose money, but most of the days we would come out on top! Pockets bulging, plenty of cash! And the ladies would be thrilling! You could afford to get laid! Grace would

be all over me again.

LINCOLN.
I thought you said she was all over you.

BOOTH.
She is she is. Im seeing her tomorrow but today we gotta solidify the shit twixt you and me. Big brother Link and little brother Booth —

LINCOLN.
3-Card.

BOOTH.
Yeah. Scheming and dreaming. No one throws the cards like you, Link. And with yr moves and my magic, and we get Grace and a girl for you to round out the posse. We'd be golden, bro! Am I right?

LINCOLN.
LINCOLN.

BOOTH.
Am I right?

LINCOLN.
I dont touch thuh cards, 3-Card. I dont touch thuh cards no more.

LINCOLN.
BOOTH.
LINCOLN.
BOOTH.

BOOTH.
You know what Mom told me when she was packing to leave? You was at school motherfucker you was at school. You got up that morning and sat down in yr regular place and read the cereal box while Dad read the sports section and Mom brought you yr dick toast and then you got on the damn school bus cause you didnt

have the sense to do nothing else you was so into yr own shit that you didnt have the sense to feel nothing else going on. I had the sense to go back cause I was feeling something going on, I was feeling something changing. So I —

LINCOLN.
Cut school that day like you did almost every day —

BOOTH.
She was putting her stuff in bags. She had all them nice suitcases but she was putting her stuff in bags.
(Rest)
Packing up her shit. She told me to look out for you. I told her I was the little brother and the big brother should look out after the little brother. She just said it again. That I should look out for you. Yeah. So who gonna look out for me. Not like you care. Here I am interested in an economic opportunity, willing to work hard, willing to take risks and all you can say you shiteating motherfucking pathetic limpdick uncle tom, all you can tell me is how you dont do no more what I be wanting to do. Here I am trying to earn a living and you standing in my way. YOU STANDING IN MY WAY, LINK!

LINCOLN.
Im sorry.

BOOTH.
Yeah, you sorry all right.

LINCOLN.
I cant be hustling no more, bro.

BOOTH.
What you do all day aint no hustle?

LINCOLN.
Its honest work.

BOOTH.
Dressing up like some crackerass white man, some dead president and letting people shoot at you sounds like a hustle to me.

LINCOLN.
People know the real deal. When people know the real deal it aint a hustle.

BOOTH.
We do the card game people will know the real deal. Sometimes we will win sometimes they will win. They fast they win, we faster we win.

LINCOLN.
I aint going back to that, bro. I aint going back.

BOOTH.
You play Honest Abe. You aint going back but you going all the way back. Back to way back then when folks was slaves and shit.

LINCOLN.
Dont push me.

BOOTH.
LINCOLN.

BOOTH.
You gonna have to leave.

LINCOLN.
I'll be gone tomorrow.

BOOTH.
Good. Cause this was only supposed to be a temporary arrangement.

LINCOLN.
I will be gone tomorrow.

BOOTH.
Good.

(Booth sits on his bed. Lincoln, sitting in his easy chair with his guitar, plays and sings.)

LINCOLN.
My dear mother left me, my fathers gone away
My dear mother left me and my fathers gone away
Aint got no money, I aint got no place to stay.

My best girl, she threw me out into the street
My favorite horse, they ground him into meat
Im feeling cold from my head down to my feet.

My luck was bad but now it turned to worse
My luck was bad but now it turned to worse
Dont call me up no doctor, just call me up a hearse.

BOOTH.
You just made that up?

LINCOLN.
I had it in my head for a few days.

BOOTH.
Sounds good.

LINCOLN.
Thanks.
(Rest)
Daddy told me once why we got the names we do.

BOOTH.
Yeah?

LINCOLN.
Yeah.

(Rest)

He was drunk when he told me, or maybe I was drunk when he told me. Anyway he told me, may not be true, but he told me. Why he named us both. Lincoln and Booth.

BOOTH.
How come. How come, man?

LINCOLN.
It was his idea of a joke.

(Both men relax back as the lights fade.)

Scene Two

Friday evening. The very next day. Booth comes in looking like he is bundled up against the cold. He makes sure his brother isnt home, then stands in the middle of the room. From his big coat sleeves he pulls out one new shoe then another, from another sleeve come two more shoes. He then slithers out a belt from each sleeve. He removes his coat. Underneath he wears a very nice new suit. He removes the jacket and pants revealing another new suit underneath. The suits still have the price tags on them. He takes two neckties and a bottle of whiskey from his pockets and two folded shirts from the back of his pants. He pulls a magazine from the front of his pants. Hes clearly had a busy day of shoplifting. He lays one suit out on Lincolns easy chair. The other he lays out on his own bed. He goes out into the hall returning with a folding screen which he sets up between the bed and the recliner creating 2 separate spaces. He sets up the whiskey and two glasses on the stacked milk crates. He hears footsteps and sits down in the small wooden chair reading the magazine. Lincoln, dressed in street clothes, comes in.

LINCOLN.
Taaaaadaaaaaaaa!

BOOTH.
Lordamighty, Pa, I smells money!

LINCOLN.
Sho nuff, Ma. Poppa done brung home thuh bacon.

BOOTH.
Bringitherebringitherebringithere.

(With a series of very elaborate moves Lincoln brings the money over to Booth.)

BOOTH.
Put it in my hands, Pa!

LINCOLN.
I want ya tuh smells it first, Ma!

BOOTH.
Put it neath my nose then, Pa!

LINCOLN.
Take yrself a good long whiff of them greenbacks.

BOOTH.
Oh lordamighty Ima faint, Pa! Get me muh med-sin!

(Lincoln quickly pours two large glasses of whiskey.)

LINCOLN.
Dont die on me, Ma!

BOOTH.
Im fading fast, Pa!

LINCOLN.
Thinka thuh children, Ma! Thinka thuh farm!

BOOTH.
1-2-3.

(Both men gulp down their drinks simultaneously.)

LINCOLN and BOOTH.
AAAAAAAAAAAAAAAAAAAAAH!

(Lots of laughing and slapping on the backs.)

LINCOLN.
Budget it out man budget it out.

BOOTH.
You in a hurry?

LINCOLN.
Yeah. I wanna see how much we got for the week.

BOOTH.
You rush in here and dont even look around. Could be a fucking
A-bomb in the middle of the floor you wouldnt notice. Yr wife,
Cookie —

LINCOLN.
X-wife —

BOOTH.
— could be in my bed you wouldnt notice —

LINCOLN.
She was once —

BOOTH.
Look the fuck around please.

(Lincoln looks around and sees the new suit on his chair.)

LINCOLN.
Wow.

BOOTH.
Its yrs.

LINCOLN.
Shit.

BOOTH.
Got myself one too.

LINCOLN.
Boosted?

BOOTH.
Yeah, I boosted em. Theys stole from a big-ass department store. That store takes in more money in one day than we will in our whole life. I stole and I stole generously. I got one for me and I got one for you. Shoes belts shirts ties socks in the shoes and everything. Got that screen too.

LINCOLN.
You all right, man.

BOOTH.
Just cause I aint good as you at cards dont mean I cant do nothing.

LINCOLN.
Lets try em on.

(They stand in their separate sleeping spaces, Booth near his bed, Lincoln near his recliner, and try on their new clothes.)

BOOTH.
Ima wear mine tonight. Gracell see me in this and *she* gonna ask

me tuh marry *her*.
(Rest)
I got you the blue and I got me the brown. I walked in there and walked out and they didnt as much as bat an eye. Thats how smooth lil bro be, Link.

LINCOLN.
You did good. You did real good, 3-Card.

BOOTH.
All in a days work.

LINCOLN.
They say the clothes make the man. All day long I wear that getup. But that dont make me who I am. Old black coat not even real old just fake old. Its got worn spots on the elbows, little raggedy places thatll break through into holes before the winters out. Shiny strips around the cuffs and the collar. Dust from the cap guns on the left shoulder where they shoot him, where they shoot me I should say but I never feel like they shooting me. The fella who had the gig before I had it wore the same coat. When I got the job they had the getup hanging there waiting for me. Said thuh fella before me just took it off one day and never came back.
(Rest)
Remember how Dads clothes used to hang in the closet?

BOOTH.
Until you took em outside and burned em.
(Rest)
He had some nice stuff. What he didnt spend on booze he spent on women. What he didnt spend on them two he spent on clothes. He had some nice stuff. I would look at his stuff and calculate thuh how long it would take till I was big enough to fit it. Then you went and burned it all up.

LINCOLN.
I got tired of looking at em without him in em.
(Rest)

They said thuh fella before me — he took off the getup one day, hung it up real nice, and never came back. And as they offered me thuh job, saying of course I would have to wear a little makeup and accept less than what they would offer a — another guy —

BOOTH.
Go on, say it. "White." Theyd pay you less than theyd pay a white guy.

LINCOLN.
I said to myself thats exactly what I would do: wear it out and then leave it hanging there and not come back. But until then, I would make a living at it. But it dont make me. Worn suit coat, not even worn by the fool that Im supposed to be playing, but making fools out of all those folks who come crowding in for they chance to play at something great. Fake beard. Top hat. Dont make me into no Lincoln. I was Lincoln on my own before any of that.

(The men finish dressing. They style and profile.)

BOOTH.
Sharp, huh?

LINCOLN.
Very sharp.

BOOTH.
You look sharp too, man. You look like the real you. Most of the time you walking around all bedraggled and shit. You look good. Like you used to look back in thuh day when you had Cookie in love with you and all the women in the world was eating out of yr hand.

LINCOLN.
This is real nice, man. I dont know where Im gonna wear it but its real nice.

BOOTH.
Just wear it around. Itll make you feel good and when you feel good yll meet someone nice. Me I aint interested in meeting no

34

one nice, I mean, I only got eyes for Grace. You think she'll go for me in this?

LINCOLN.
I think thuh tie you gave me'll go better with what you got on.

BOOTH.
Yeah?

LINCOLN.
Grace likes bright colors dont she? My ties bright, yrs is too subdued.

BOOTH.
Yeah. Gimmie yr tie.

LINCOLN.
You gonna take back a gift?

BOOTH.
I stole the damn thing didnt I? Gimmie yrs! I'll give you mines.

(They switch neckties. Booth is pleased. Lincoln is more pleased.)

LINCOLN.
Do thuh budget.

BOOTH.
Right. Ok lets see: we got 314 dollars. We put 100 aside for the rent. 100 a week times 4 weeks makes the rent and —

LINCOLN and BOOTH.
— we dont want thuh rent spent.

BOOTH.
That leaves 214. We put aside 30 for the electric leaving 184. We put aside 50 for thuh phone leaving 134.

35

LINCOLN.
We dont got a phone.

BOOTH.
We pay our bill theyll turn it back on.

LINCOLN.
We dont need no phone.

BOOTH.
How you gonna get a woman if you dont got a phone? Women these days are more cautious, more whaddacallit, more circum-spect. You go into a club looking like a fast daddy, you get a filly to give you her numerophono and gone is the days when she just gives you her number and dont ask for yrs.

LINCOLN.
Like a woman is gonna call me.

BOOTH.
She dont wanna call you she just doing a preliminary survey of the property. Shit, Link, you dont know nothin no more.
(Rest)
She gives you her number and she asks for yrs. You give her yr number. The phone number of yr home. Thereby telling her 3 things: 1) you got a home, that is, you aint no smooth talking smooth dressing *homeless* joe; 2) that you is in possession of a tele-phone and a working telephone number which is to say that you got thuh cash and thuh wherewithal to acquire for yr self the worlds most revolutionary communication apparatus and you together enough to pay yr bills!

LINCOLN.
Whats 3?

BOOTH.
You give her yr number you telling her that its cool to call if she should so please, that is, that you aint got no wife or wife approx-

imation on the premises.
(Rest)
50 for the phone leaving 134. We put aside 40 for "med-sin."

LINCOLN.
The price went up. 2 bucks more a bottle.

BOOTH.
We'll put aside 50, then. That covers the bills. We got 84 left. 40 for meals together during the week leaving 44. 30 for me 14 for you. I got a woman I gotta impress tonight.

LINCOLN.
You didnt take out for the phone last week.

BOOTH.
Last week I was depressed. This week things is looking up. For both of us.

LINCOLN.
Theyre talking about cutbacks at the arcade. I only been there 8 months, so —

BOOTH.
Dont sweat it man, we'll find something else.

LINCOLN.
Not nothing like this. I like the job. This is sit down, you know, easy work. I just gotta sit there all day. Folks come in kill phony Honest Abe with the phony pistol. I can sit there and let my mind travel.

BOOTH.
Think of women.

LINCOLN.
Sometimes.
(Rest)
All around the whole arcade is buzzing and popping. Thuh

whirring of thuh duckshoot, baseballs smacking the back wall
when someone misses the stack of cans, some woman getting
happy cause her fella just won the ring toss. The Boss playing the
barker talking up the fake freaks. The smell of the ocean and cot-
ton candy and rat shit. And in thuh middle of all that, I can just
sit and let my head go quiet. Make up songs, make plans. Forget.
(Rest)
You should come down again.

BOOTH.
Once was plenty, but thanks.
(Rest)
Yr Best Customer, he come in today?

LINCOLN.
Oh, yeah, he was there.

BOOTH.
He shoot you?

LINCOLN.
He shot Honest Abe, yeah.

BOOTH.
He talk to you?

LINCOLN.
In a whisper. Shoots on the left whispers on the right.

BOOTH.
Whatd he say this time?

LINCOLN.
"Does thuh show stop when no ones watching or does thuh show
go on?"

BOOTH.
Hes getting deep.

LINCOLN.
Yeah.

BOOTH.
Whatd he say, that one time? "Yr only yrself — "

LINCOLN.
" — when no ones watching," yeah.

BOOTH.
Thats deep shit.
(Rest)
Hes a brother, right?

LINCOLN.
I think so.

BOOTH.
He know yr a brother?

LINCOLN.
I dunno.

BOOTH.
Hes a *deep* black brother.

LINCOLN.
Yeah. He makes the day interesting.

BOOTH.
(Rest)
Thats a fucked-up job you got.

LINCOLN.
Its a living.

BOOTH.
But you aint living.

LINCOLN.
Im alive aint I?
(Rest)
One day I was throwing the cards. Next day Lonny died. Somebody shot him. I knew I was next, so I quit. I saved my life.
(Rest)
The arcade gig is the first lucky break Ive ever had. And Ive actually grown to like the work. And now theyre talking about cutting me.

BOOTH.
You was lucky with thuh cards.

LINCOLN.
Lucky? Aint nothing lucky about thuh cards. Cards aint luck. Cards is work. Cards is skill. Aint never nothing lucky about thuh cards.
(Rest)
I dont wanna lose my job.

BOOTH.
Then you gotta jazz up yr act. Elaborate yr moves, you know. You was always too stiff with it. You cant just sit there! Maybe, when they shoot you, you know, leap up flail yr arms then fall down and wiggle around and shit so they gotta shoot you more than once. Blam Blam Blam! Blam!

LINCOLN.
Help me practice. I'll sit here like I do at work and you be like one of the tourists.

BOOTH.
No thanks.

LINCOLN.
My paychecks on the line, man.

BOOTH.
I got a date. Practice on yr own.
(Rest)

I got a rendezvous with Grace. Shit she so sweet she makes my teeth hurt.
(Rest)
Link, uh, howbout slipping me an extra 5 spot. Its the biggest night of my life.

LINCOLN.
BOOTH.

(Lincoln gives Booth a 5er.)

BOOTH.
Thanks.

LINCOLN.
No sweat.

BOOTH.
Howabout I run through it with you when I get back. Put on yr getup and practice till then.

LINCOLN.
Sure.

(Booth leaves. Lincoln stands there alone. He takes off his shoes, giving them a shine. He takes off his socks and his fancy suit, hanging it neatly over the little wooden chair. He takes his getup out of his shopping bag. He puts it on, slowly, like an actor preparing for a great role: frock coat, pants, beard, top hat, necktie. He leaves his feet bare. The top hat has an elastic band which he positions securely underneath his chin. He picks up the white pancake makeup but decides against it. He sits. He pretends to get shot, flings himself on the floor and thrashes around. He gets up, considers giving the new moves another try, but instead pours himself a big glass of whiskey and sits there drinking.)

Scene Three

Much later that same Friday evening. The recliner is extended to its maximum horizontal position and Lincoln lies there asleep. He wakes with a start. He is horrific, bleary eyed and hungover, in his full Lincoln regalia. He takes a deep breath, realizes where he is and reclines again, going back to sleep. Booth comes in full of swagger. He slams the door trying to wake his brother who is dead to the world. He opens the door and slams it again. This time Lincoln wakes up, as hungover and horrid as before. Booth swaggers about, his moves are exaggerated, rooster-like. He walks round and round Lincoln making sure his brother sees him.

LINCOLN.
You hurt yrself?

BOOTH.
I had me "an evening to remember."

LINCOLN.
You look like you hurt yrself.

BOOTH.
Grace Grace Grace. *Grace.* She wants me back. She wants me back so bad she wiped her hand over the past where we wasnt together just so she could say we aint never been apart. She wiped her hand over our breakup. She wiped her hand over her childhood, her teenage years, her first boyfriend, just so she could say that she been mine since the dawn of time.

LINCOLN.
Thats great, man.

BOOTH.
And all the shit I put her through: she wiped it clean. And all the
women I saw while I was seeing her —

LINCOLN.
Wiped clean too?

BOOTH.
Mister Clean, Mister, Mister Clean!

LINCOLN.
Whered you take her?

BOOTH.
We was over at her place. I brought thuh food. Stopped at the best
place I could find and stuffed my coat with only the best. We had
the music we had the candlelight we had —

LINCOLN.
She let you do it?

BOOTH.
Course she let me do it.

LINCOLN.
She let you do it without a rubber?

BOOTH.
— Yeah.

LINCOLN.
Bullshit.

BOOTH.
I put my foot down — and she *melted*. And she was — huh — she
was something else. I dont wanna get you jealous, though.

LINCOLN.
Go head, I dont mind.

BOOTH.
(Rest)
Well, you know what she looks like.

LINCOLN.
She walks on by and the emergency room fills up cause all the guys
get whiplash from lookin at her.

BOOTH.
Thats right thats right. Well — she comes to the door wearing
nothing but her little nightie, eats up the food I'd brought like
there was no tomorrow and then goes and eats on me.
(Rest)

LINCOLN.
Go on.

BOOTH.
I dont wanna make you feel bad, man.

LINCOLN.
Ssallright. Go on.

BOOTH.
(Rest)
Well, uh, you know what shes like. Wild. Goodlooking. So sweet
my teeth hurt.

LINCOLN.
A sexmachine.

BOOTH.
Yeah.

LINCOLN.
A hotsy-totsy.

BOOTH.
Yeah.

LINCOLN.
Amazing Grace.

BOOTH.
Amazing Grace! Yeah. Thats right. She let me do her how I wanted.
And no rubber.
(Rest)

LINCOLN.
Go on.

BOOTH.
You dont wanna hear the mushy shit.

LINCOLN.
Sure I do.

BOOTH.
You hate the mushy shit. You always hated the mushy shit.

LINCOLN.
Ive changed. Go head. You had "an evening to remember,"
remember? I was just here alone sitting here. Drinking. Go head.
Tell Link thuh stink
(Rest)
Howd ya do her?

BOOTH.
Dogstyle.

LINCOLN.
Amazing Grace.

BOOTH.
In front of a mirror.

LINCOLN.
So you could see her. Her face her breasts her back her ass. Graces got a great ass.

BOOTH.
Its all right.

LINCOLN.
Amazing Grace!

(Booth goes into his bed area and takes off his suit, tossing the clothes on the floor.)

BOOTH.
She said next time Ima have to use a rubber. She let me have my way this time but she said that next time I'd have to put my boots on.

LINCOLN.
Im sure you can talk her out of it.

BOOTH.
Yeah.
(Rest)
What kind of rubbers you use, I mean, when you was with Cookie.

LINCOLN.
We didnt use rubbers. We was married, man.

BOOTH.
Right. But you had other women on the side. What kind you use when you was with them?

LINCOLN.
Magnums.

BOOTH.
Thats thuh kind I picked up. For next time. Grace was real strict about it. Magnums.

(While Booth sits on his bed fiddling with his box of condoms, Lincoln sits in his chair and resumes drinking.)

LINCOLN.
Theyre for "the larger man."

BOOTH.
Right. Right.

(Lincoln keeps drinking as Booth, sitting in the privacy of his bedroom, flips through a girlie magazine.)

LINCOLN.
Thats right.

BOOTH.
Graces real different from them fly-by-night gals I was making do with. Shes in school. Making something of herself. Studying cosmetology. You should see what she can do with a womans hair and nails.

LINCOLN.
Too bad you aint a woman.

BOOTH.
What?

LINCOLN.
You could get yrs done for free, I mean.

BOOTH.
Yeah. She got this way of sitting. Of talking. That. Everything she does is. Shes just so hot.
(Rest)
We was together 2 years. Then we broke up. I had my little employ-

ment difficulty and she needed time to think.

LINCOLN.
And shes through thinking now.

BOOTH.
Thats right.

LINCOLN.
BOOTH.

LINCOLN.
Whatcha doing back there?

BOOTH.
Resting. That girl wore me out.

LINCOLN.
You want some med-sin?

BOOTH.
No thanks.

LINCOLN.
Come practice my moves with me, then.

BOOTH.
Lets hit it tomorrow, K?

LINCOLN.
I been waiting. I got all dressed up and you said if I waited up —
come on, man, they gonna replace me with a wax dummy.

BOOTH.
No shit.

LINCOLN.
Thats what theyre talking about. Probably just talk, but — come

on, man, I even lent you 5 bucks.

BOOTH.
Im tired.

LINCOLN.
BOOTH.

LINCOLN.
You didnt get shit tonight.

BOOTH.
You jealous, man. You just jail-us.

LINCOLN.
You laying over there yr balls blue as my boosted suit. Laying over there waiting for me to go back to sleep or black out so I wont hear you rustling thuh pages of yr fuck book.

BOOTH.
Fuck you, man.

LINCOLN.
I was over there looking for something the other week and theres like 100 fuck books under yr bed and theyre matted together like a bad fro, bro, cause you spunked in the pages and didnt wipe them off.

BOOTH.
Im hot. I need constant sexual release. If I wasnt taking care of myself by myself I would be out there running around on thuh town which costs cash that I dont have so I would be doing worse: I'd be out there doing who knows what, shooting people and shit. Out of a need for unresolved sexual release. Im a hot man. I aint apologizing for it. When I dont got a woman, I gotta make do. Not like you, Link. When you dont got a woman you just sit there. Letting yr shit fester. Yr dick, if it aint falled off yet, is hanging there between yr legs, little whiteface shriveled-up blank-shooting grub worm. As goes thuh man so goes thuh mans dick.

Thats what I say. Least my shits intact.
(Rest)
You a limp dick jealous whiteface motherfucker whose wife dumped him cause he couldnt get it up and she told me so. Came crawling to me cause she needed a man.
(Rest)
I gave it to Grace good tonight. So goodnight.

LINCOLN.
(Rest)
Goodnight.

LINCOLN.
BOOTH.
LINCOLN.
BOOTH.
LINCOLN.
BOOTH.

(Lincoln sitting in his chair. Booth lying in bed. Time passes. Booth peeks out to see if Lincoln is asleep. Lincoln is watching for him.)

LINCOLN.
You can hustle 3-card monte without me you know.

BOOTH.
Im planning to.

LINCOLN.
I could contact my old crew. You could work with them. Lonny aint around no more but theres the rest of them. Theyre good.

BOOTH.
I can get my own crew. I dont need yr crew. Buncha hasbeens. I can get my own crew.

LINCOLN.
My crews experienced. We usedta pull down a thousand a day.

50

Thats 7 G a week. That was years ago. They probably do twice, 3 times that now.

BOOTH.
I got my own connections, thank you.

LINCOLN.
Theyd take you on in a heartbeat. With my say. My say still counts with them. They know you from before, when you tried to hang with us but — wernt ready yet. They know you from then, but I'd talk you up. I'd say yr my bro, which they know, and I'd say youd been working the west coast. Little towns. Mexican border. Taking tourists. I'd tell them you got moves like I dreamed of having. Meanwhile youd be working out yr shit right here, right in this room, getting good and getting better every day so when I did do the reintroductions youd have some marketable skills. Youd be passable.

BOOTH.
I'd be more than passable, I'd be the be all end all.

LINCOLN.
Youd be the be all end all. And youd have my say. If yr interested.

BOOTH.
Could do.

LINCOLN.
Youd have to get a piece. They all pack pistols, bro.

BOOTH.
I *got* a piece.

LINCOLN.
Youd have to be packing something more substantial than that pop gun, 3-Card. These hustlers is upper echelon hustlers they pack upper echelon heat, not no Saturday night shit, now.

BOOTH.
Whata you know of heat? You aint hung with those guys for 6, 7 years. You swore off em. Threw yr heat in thuh river and you "Dont touch thuh cards." I know more about heat than you know about heat.

LINCOLN.
Im around guns every day. At the arcade. Theyve all been reworked so they only fire caps but I see guns every day. Lots of guns.

BOOTH.
What kinds?

LINCOLN.
You been there, you seen them. Shiny deadly metal each with their own deadly personality.

BOOTH.
Maybe I *could* visit you over there. I'd boost one of them guns and rework it to make it shoot for real again. What kind you think would best suit my personality?

LINCOLN.
You aint stealing nothing from the arcade.

BOOTH.
I go in there and steal I wanna go in there and steal I go in there and steal.

LINCOLN.
It aint worth it. They dont shoot nothing but blanks.

BOOTH.
Yeah, like you. Shooting blanks.
(Rest)
(Rest)
You ever wonder if someones gonna come in there with a real gun? A real gun with real slugs? Someone with uh axe tuh grind or

something?

LINCOLN.
No.

BOOTH.
Someone who hates you come in there and guns you down and gets gone before anybody finds out.

LINCOLN.
I dont got no enemies.

BOOTH.
Yr X.

LINCOLN.
Cookie dont hate me.

BOOTH.
Yr Best Customer? Some miscellaneous stranger?

LINCOLN.
I cant be worrying about the actions of miscellaneous strangers.

BOOTH.
But there they come day in day out for a chance to shoot Honest Abe.
(Rest)
Who are they mostly?

LINCOLN.
I dont really look.

BOOTH.
You must see something.

LINCOLN.
Im supposed to be staring straight ahead. Watching a play, like

Abe was.

BOOTH.
All day goes by and you never take a sneak peek at who be pulling the trigger.

(Pulled in by his own curiosity, Booth has come out of his bed area to stand on the dividing line between the two spaces.)

LINCOLN.
Its pretty dark. To keep thuh illusion of thuh whole thing.
(Rest)
But on thuh wall opposite where I sit theres a little electrical box, like a fuse box. Silver metal. Its got uh dent in it like somebody hit it with they fist. Big old dent so everything reflected in it gets reflected upside down. Like yr looking in uh spoon. And thats where I can see em. The assassins.
(Rest)
Not behind me yet but I can hear him coming. Coming in with his gun in hand, thuh gun he already picked out up front when he paid his fare. Coming on in. But not behind me yet. His dress shoes making too much noise on the carpet, the carpets too thin, Boss should get a new one but hes cheap. Not behind me yet. Not behind me yet. Cheap lightbulb just above my head.
(Rest)
And there he is. Standing behind me. Standing in position. Standing upside down. Theres some feet shapes on the floor so he knows just where he oughta stand. So he wont miss. Thuh gun is always cold. Winter or summer thuh gun is always cold. And when the gun touches me he can feel that Im warm and he knows Im alive. And if Im alive then he can shoot me dead. And for a minute, with him hanging back there behind me, its real. Me looking at him upside down and him looking at me looking like Lincoln. Then he shoots.
(Rest)
I slump down and close my eyes. And he goes out thuh other way. More come in. Uh whole day full. Bunches of kids, little good for nothings, in they school uniforms. Businessmen smelling like two

for one martinis. Tourists in they theme park t-shirts trying to catch it all on film. Housewives with they mouths closed tight, shooting more than once.

(Rest)

They all get so into it. I do my best for them. And now they talking bout cutting me, replacing me with uh wax dummy.

BOOTH.
You just gotta show yr boss that you can do things a wax dummy cant do. You too dry with it. You gotta add spicy shit.

LINCOLN.
Like what.

BOOTH.
Like when they shoot you, I dunno, scream or something.

LINCOLN.
Scream?

(Booth plays the killer without using his gun.)

BOOTH.
Try it. I'll be the killer. Bang!

LINCOLN.
Aaaah!

BOOTH.
Thats good.

LINCOLN.
A wax dummy can scream. They can put a voicebox in it and make it like its screaming.

BOOTH.
You can curse. Try it. Bang!

LINCOLN.
Motherfucking cocksucker!

BOOTH.
Thats good, man.

LINCOLN.
They aint going for that, though.

BOOTH.
You practice rolling and wiggling on the floor?

LINCOLN.
A little.

BOOTH.
Lemmie see. Bang!

(Lincoln slumps down, falls on the floor and silently wiggles around.)

BOOTH.
You look more like a worm on the sidewalk. Move yr arms. Good.
Now scream or something.

LINCOLN.
Aaaah! Aaaaah! Aaaah!

BOOTH.
A little tougher than that, you sound like yr fucking.

LINCOLN.
Aaaaaah!

BOOTH.
Hold yr head or something, where I shotcha. Good. And look at
me! I am the assassin! *I am Booth!!* Come on man this is life and
death! Go all out!

(Lincoln goes all out.)

BOOTH.
Cool, man thats cool. Thats enough.

LINCOLN.
Whatdoyathink?

BOOTH.
I dunno, man. Something about it. I dunno. It was looking too real or something.

LINCOLN.
Goddamn you! They dont want it looking too real. I'd scare the customers. Then I'd be out for sure. Yr trying to get me fired.

BOOTH.
Im trying to help. Cross my heart.

LINCOLN.
People are funny about they Lincoln shit. Its historical. People like they historical shit in a certain way. They like it to unfold the way they folded it up. Neatly like a book. Not raggedy and bloody and screaming. You trying to get me fired.
(Rest)
I am uh brother playing Lincoln. Its uh stretch for anyones imagination. And it aint easy for me neither. Every day I put on that shit, I leave my own shit at the door and I put on that shit and I go out there and I make it work. I make it look easy but its hard. That shit is hard. But it works. Cause I work it. And you trying to get me fired.
(Rest)
I swore off them cards. Took nowhere jobs. Drank. Then Cookie threw me out. What thuh fuck was I gonna do? I seen that "Help Wanted" sign and I went up in there and I looked good in the getup and agreed to the whiteface and they really dug it that me and Honest Abe got the same name.
(Rest)

Its a sit down job. With benefits. I dont wanna get fired. They wont give me a good reference if I get fired.

BOOTH.
Iffen you was tuh get fired, then, well — then you and me could — hustle the cards together. We'd have to support ourselves somehow.
(Rest)
Just show me how to do the hook part of the card hustle, man. The part where the Dealer looks away but somehow he sees —

LINCOLN.
I couldnt remember if I wanted to.

BOOTH.
Sure you could.

LINCOLN.
NO!
(Rest)
Night, man.

BOOTH.
Yeah.

(Lincoln stretches out in his recliner. Booth stands over him waiting for him to get up, to change his mind. But Lincoln is fast asleep. Booth covers him with a blanket then goes to his bed, turning off the lights as he goes. He quietly rummages underneath his bed for a girlie magazine which, as the lights fade, he reads with great interest.)

Scene Four

Saturday. Just before dawn. Lincoln gets up. Looks around. Booth is fast asleep, dead to the world.

LINCOLN.
No fucking running water.

(He stumbles around the room looking for something which he finally finds: a plastic cup, which he uses as a urinal. He finishes peeing and finds an out of the way place to stow the cup. He claws at his Lincoln getup, removing it and tearing it in the process. He strips down to his t-shirt and shorts.)

LINCOLN.
Hate falling asleep in this damn shit. Shit. Ripped the beard. I can just hear em tomorrow. Busiest day of the week. They looking me over to make sure Im presentable. They got a slew of guys working but Im the only one they look over every day. "Yr beards ripped, pal. Sure, we'll getcha new one but its gonna be coming outa yr pay." Shit. I should quit right then and there. I'd yank off the beard, throw it on the ground and stomp it, then go strangle the fucking boss. Thatd be good. My hands around his neck and his bug eyes bugging out. You been ripping me off since I took this job and now Im gonna have to take it outa *yr* pay, motherfucker. Shit.
(Rest)
Sit down job. With benefits.
(Rest)
Hustling. Shit, I was good. I was great. Hell I was the be all end all. I was throwing cards like throwing cards was made for me. Made for me and me alone. I was the best anyone ever seen. Coast to coast. Everybody said so. And I never lost. Not once. Not one time. Not never. Thats how much them cards was mines. I was the be all end all. I was that good.
(Rest)
Then you woke up one day and you didnt have the taste for it no more. Like something in you knew — . Like something in you knew it was time to quit. Quit while you was still ahead. Something in you was telling you — . But hells no. Not Link thuh stink. So I went out there and threw one more time. What thuh fuck. And Lonny died.
(Rest)
Got yrself a good job. And when the arcade lets you go yll get

another good job. I dont gotta spend my whole life hustling. Theres more to Link than that. More to me than some cheap hustle. More to life than cheating some idiot out of his paycheck or his life savings.
(Rest)
Like that joker and his wife from out of town. Always wanted to see the big city. I said you could see the bigger end of the big city with a little more cash. And if they was fast enough, faster than me, and here I slowed down my moves I slowed em way down and my Lonny, my right hand, my Stickman, Lonny could draw a customer in like nothing else, Lonny could draw a fly from fresh shit, he could draw Adam outa Eve just with that look he had, Lonny always got folks playing.
(Rest)
Somebody shot him. They dont know who. Nobody knows nobody cares.
(Rest)
We took that man and his wife for hundreds. No, thousands. We took them for everything they had and everything they ever wanted to have. We took a father for the money he was gonna get his kids new bike with and he cried in the street while we vanished. We took a mothers welfare check, she pulled a knife on us and we ran. She threw it but her aim werent shit. People shopping. Greedy. Thinking they could take me and they got took instead.
(Rest)
Swore off thuh cards. Something inside me telling me — . But I was good.

LINCOLN.
LINCOLN.

(He sees a packet of cards. He studies them like an alcoholic would study a drink. Then he reaches for them, but chooses not to pick them up. Instead he simply stands over the monte setup, pretending.)

LINCOLN.
Still got my moves. Still got my touch. Still got my chops. Thuh feel of it. And I aint hurting no one, God. Link is just here hustling hisself.

(Rest)
Lets see whatcha got.

(He moves "the cards" slowly at first, aimlessly, as if hes just making little ripples in water. But the game has a strong undertow, and draws him deeper into it.)

LINCOLN.
(((Lean in close and watch me now: who see thuh black card who see thuh black card I see thuh black card black cards thuh winner pick thuh black card thats thuh winner pick thuh red card thats thuh loser pick thuh other red card thats thuh other loser pick thuh black card you pick thuh winner. Watch me as I throw thuh cards. Here we go.)))

(Even though Lincoln speaks softly, Booth wakes and, unbeknownst to Lincoln, listens intently.)

(((Who see thuh black card who see thuh black card? You pick thuh red card you pick a loser you pick that red card you pick a loser you pick thuh black card thuh deuce of spades you pick a winner who sees thuh deuce of spades thuh one who sees it never fades watch me now as I throw thuh cards. Red losers black winner follow thuh deuce of spades chase thuh black deuce. Dark deuce will get you thuh win.)))

(Rest)
LINCOLN.
((10 will get you 20, 20 will get you 40.))

(The pull of the game is very strong. Suddenly, hes like a junkie needing his fix. Nothing else is as important as getting his hands on those cards again. Its as if the cards are playing him. He breaks, snatching up the deck, picking out 3 cards and throwing them down.)

((Ima show you thuh cards: 2 red cards but only one spade. Dark winner in thuh center and thuh red losers on thuh sides. Pick uh red card you got a loser pick thuh other red card you got a loser pick

thuh black card you got a winner. One good pickll get you in, 2 good picks and you gone win. Watch me come on watch me now.))
(Rest)
((Who sees thuh winner who knows where its at? You do? You sure? Go on then, put yr money where yr mouth is. Put yr money down you aint no clown. No? Ah, you had thuh card but you didnt have thuh heart.))
(Rest)
((Watch me now as I throw thuh cards watch me real close. Ok, man, you know which card is the deuce of spades? Was you watching Links lighting fast express? Was you watching Link cause he the best? So you sure, huh? Point it out first, then place yr bet and Linkll show you yr winner.))
(Rest)
((500 dollars? You thuh man of thuh hour you thuh man with thuh power. You musta been watching Link real close. You must be thuh man who know thuh most. Ok. Lay the cash in my hand cause Link the man. Thank you, mister. This card you say?))
(Rest)
((Wrong! Ha!))
(Rest)
((Thats thuh show. We gotta go.))
(Knowing hes in too deep, Lincoln drops the cards and quickly moves away from the monte setup. He stands a safe distance away, at the edge of his easy chair, but he cant take his eyes off the game.)
[LINCOLN.
God help me.]

Scene Five

Several days have passed. Its now Wednesday night. Booth is sitting in his brand-new suit. The monte setup is nowhere in sight. In its place is a table with two nice chairs. The table is covered with a lovely tablecloth and there are nice plates, silverware, champagne glasses and candles. All the makings of a very romantic dinner for two. The whole apartment in fact takes its cue from the table. Its been cleaned up considerably. New curtains on the windows, a doily-like object on the recliner. Booth sits at the table darting his eyes around, making sure everything is looking good.

BOOTH.
Shit.

(He notices some of his girlie magazines visible from underneath his bed. He goes over and nudges them out of sight. He sits back down. He notices that theyre still visible. He goes over and nudges them some more, kicking at them finally. Then he takes the spread from his bed and pulls it down, hiding them. He sits back down. He gets up. Checks the champagne on much melted ice. Checks the food.)

BOOTH.
Foods getting cold, Grace!! Dont worry man, she'll get here, she'll get here.

(He sits back down. He goes over to the bed. Checks it for springiness. Smoothes down the bedspread. Double-checks 2 matching silk dressing gowns, very expensive, marked "His" and "Hers." Lays the dressing gowns across the bed again. He sits back down. He cant help but notice the visibility of the girlie magazines again. He goes to the bed, kicks them fiercely, then on his hands and knees shoves them. Then he begins to get under the bed to push them, but he remembers his nice clothing and takes off his jacket. After a beat he removes his pants and, in this half-dressed way, he crawls under the bed to give those telltale magazines a good and final shove. Lincoln comes in. At first Booth, still stripped down to his underwear, thinks its his date. When he realizes its his brother, he does his best to keep Lincoln from entering the apartment. Lincoln wears his frock coat and carries the rest of his getup in a plastic bag.)

LINCOLN.
You in the middle of it?

BOOTH.
What the hell you doing here?

LINCOLN.
If yr in thuh middle of it I can go. Or I can just be real quiet and just — sing a song in my head or something.

BOOTH.
The casas off limits to you tonight.

LINCOLN.
You know when we lived in that 2-room place with the cement backyard and the frontyard with nothing but trash in it, Mom and Pops would do it in the middle of the night and I would always hear them but I would sing in my head, cause, I dunno, I couldnt bear to listen.

BOOTH.
You gotta get out of here.

LINCOLN.
I would make up all kinds of songs. Oh, sorry, yr all up in it. No sweat, bro. No sweat. Hey, Grace, howyadoing?!

BOOTH.
She aint here yet, man. Shes running late. And its a good thing too cause I aint all dressed yet. Yr gonna spend thuh night with friends?

LINCOLN.
Yeah.

(Booth waits for Lincoln to leave. Lincoln stands his ground.)

LINCOLN.
I lost my job.

BOOTH.
Hunh.

LINCOLN.
I come in there right on time like I do every day and that mother-fucker gives me some song and dance about cutbacks and too many folks complaining.

BOOTH.
Hunh.

LINCOLN.
Showd me thuh wax dummy — hes buying it right out of a catalog.
(Rest)
I walked out still wearing my getup.
(Rest)
I could go back in tomorrow. I could tell him I'll take another pay cut. Thatll get him to take me back.

BOOTH.
Link. Yr free. Dont go crawling back. Yr free at last! Now you can do anything you want. Yr not tied down by that job. You can — you can do something else. Something that pays better maybe.

LINCOLN.
You mean Hustle.

BOOTH.
Maybe. Hey, Graces on her way. You gotta go.

(Lincoln flops into his chair. Booth is waiting for him to move. Lincoln doesnt budge.)

LINCOLN.
I'll stay until she gets here. I'll act nice. I wont embarrass you.

BOOTH.
You gotta go.

LINCOLN.
What time she coming?

BOOTH.
Shes late. She could be here any second.

LINCOLN.
I'll meet her. I met her years ago. I'll meet her again.
(Rest)
How late is she?

BOOTH.
She was supposed to be here at 8.

LINCOLN.
Its after 2 a.m. Shes — shes late.
(Rest)
Maybe when she comes you could put the blanket over me and I'll
just pretend like Im not here.
(Rest)
I'll wait. And when she comes I'll go. I need to sit down. I been
walking around all day.

BOOTH.
LINCOLN.

(Booth goes to his bed and dresses hurriedly.)

BOOTH.
Pretty nice, right? The china thuh silver thuh crystal.

LINCOLN.
Its great.
(Rest)
Boosted?

BOOTH.
Yeah.

LINCOLN.
Thought you went and spent yr inheritance for a minute, you had

66

me going I was thinking shit, Booth — 3-Card — that 3-Cards gone and spent his inheritance and the gal is — late.

BOOTH.
Its boosted. Every bit of it.
(Rest)
Fuck this waiting bullshit.

LINCOLN.
She'll be here in a minute. Dont sweat it.

BOOTH.
Right.

(Booth comes to the table. Sits. Relaxes as best he can.)

BOOTH.
How come I got a hand for boosting and I dont got a hand for throwing cards? Its sorta the same thing — you gotta be quick — and slick. Maybe yll show me yr moves sometime.

LINCOLN.
BOOTH.
LINCOLN.
BOOTH.

LINCOLN.
Look out the window. When you see Grace coming, I'll go.

BOOTH.
Cool. Cause youd jinx it, youd really jinx it. Maybe you being here has jinxed it already. Naw. Shes just a little late. You aint jinxed nothing.

(Booth sits by the window, glancing out, watching for his date. Lincoln sits in his recliner. He finds the whiskey bottle, sips from it. He then rummages around, finding the raggedy photo album. He looks through it.

LINCOLN.
There we are at that house. Remember when we moved in?

BOOTH.
No.

LINCOLN.
You were 2 or 3.

BOOTH.
I was 4.

LINCOLN.
I was 9. We all thought it was the best fucking house in the world.

BOOTH.
Cement backyard and a frontyard full of trash, yeah, dont be going down memory lane man, yll jinx thuh vibe I got going in here. Gracell be walking in here and wrinkling up her nose cause you done jinxed up thuh joint with yr raggedy recollections.

LINCOLN.
We had some great times in that house, bro. Selling lemonade on thuh corner, thuh treehouse out back, summers spent lying in thuh grass and looking at thuh stars.

BOOTH.
We never did none of that shit.

LINCOLN.
But we had us some good times. That row of nails I got you to line up behind Dads car so when he backed out the drive-way to work —

BOOTH.
He came back that night, only time I ever seen his face go red, 4 flat tires and yelling bout how thuh white man done sabotaged him again.

LINCOLN.
And neither of us flinched. Neither of us let on that itd been us.

BOOTH.
It was at dinner, right? What were we eating?

LINCOLN.
Food.

BOOTH.
We was eating pork chops, mashed potatoes and peas. I remember cause I had to look at them peas real hard to keep from letting on. And I would glance over at you, not really glancing not actually turning my head, but I was looking at you out thuh corner of my eye. I was sure he was gonna find us out and then he woulda whipped us good. But I kept glancing at you and you was cool, man. Like nothing was going on. You was cooooool.
(Rest)
What time is it?

LINCOLN.
After 3.
(Rest)
You should call her. Something mighta happened.

BOOTH.
No man, Im cool. She'll be here in a minute. Patience is a virtue. She'll be here.

LINCOLN.
You look sad.

BOOTH.
Nope. Im just, you know, Im just —

LINCOLN.
Cool.

BOOTH.
Yeah. Cool.

(Booth comes over, takes the bottle of whiskey and pours himself a big glassful. He returns to the window looking out and drinking.)

BOOTH.
They give you a severance package, at thuh job?

LINCOLN.
A weeks pay.

BOOTH.
Great.

LINCOLN.
I blew it. Spent it all.

BOOTH.
On what?

LINCOLN.
— Just spent it.
(Rest)
It felt good, spending it. Felt really good. Like back in thuh day when I was really making money. Throwing thuh cards all day and strutting and rutting all night. Didnt have to take no shit from no fool, didnt have to worry about getting fired in favor of some damn wax dummy. I was thuh shit and they was my fools.
(Rest)
Back in thuh day.
(Rest)
(Rest)
Why you think they left us, man?

BOOTH.
Mom and Pops? I dont think about it too much.

LINCOLN.
I dont think they liked us.

BOOTH.
Naw. That aint it.

LINCOLN.
I think there was something out there that they liked more than
they liked us and for years they was struggling against moving
towards that more liked something. Each of them had a special
something that they was struggling against. Moms had hers. Pops
had his. And they was struggling. We moved out of that nasty
apartment into a house. A whole house. It wernt perfect but it was
a house and theyd bought it and they brought us there and everything we owned, figuring we could be a family in that house and
them things, them two separate things each of them was struggling
against, would just leave them be. Them things would see thuh
house and be impressed and just leave them be. Would see thuh
job Pops had and how he shined his shoes every night before he
went to bed, shining them shoes whether they needed it or not,
and thuh thing he was struggling against would see all that and
just let him be, and thuh thing Moms was struggling against, it
would see the food on the table every night and listen to her voice
when she'd read to us sometimes, the clean clothes, the buttons
sewed on all right and it would just let her be. Just let us all be,
just regular people living in a house. That wernt too much to ask.

BOOTH.
Least we was grown when they split.

LINCOLN.
16 and 11 aint grown.

BOOTH.
16s grown. Almost. And I was ok cause you was there.
(Rest)
Shit man, it aint like they both one day both, together packed all
they shit up and left us so they could have fun in thuh sun on

71

some tropical island and you and me would have to grub in thuh dirt forever. They didnt leave together. That makes it different. She left. 2 years go by. Then he left. Like neither of them couldnt handle it no more. She split then he split. Like thuh whole family mortgage bills going to work thing was just too much. And I dont blame them. You dont see me holding down a steady job. Cause its bullshit and I know it. I seen how it cracked them up and I aint going there.

(Rest)

It aint right me trying to make myself into a one woman man just cause Grace wants me like that. One woman rubber-wearing motherfucker. Shit. Not me. She gonna walk in here looking all hot and shit trying to see how much she can get me to sweat, how much she can get me to give her before she gives me mines. Shit.

LINCOLN.
BOOTH.

LINCOLN.
Moms told me I shouldnt never get married.

BOOTH.
She told me thuh same thing.

LINCOLN.
They gave us each 500 bucks then they cut out.

BOOTH.
Thats what Im gonna do. Give my kids 500 bucks then cut out. Thats thuh way to do it.

LINCOLN.
You dont got no kids.

BOOTH.
Im gonna have kids then Im gonna cut out.

LINCOLN.
Leaving each of yr offspring 500 bucks as yr splitting.

BOOTH.
Yeah.
(Rest)
Just goes to show Mom and Pops had some agreement between them.

LINCOLN.
How so.

BOOTH.
Theyd stopped talking to eachother. Theyd stopped *screwing* eachother. But they had an agreement. Somewhere in there when it looked like all they had was hate they sat down and did thuh "split" budget.
(Rest)
When Moms splits she gives me 5 hundred-dollar bills rolled up and tied up tight in one of her nylon stockings. She tells me to put it in a safe place, to spend it only in case of an emergency, and not to tell nobody I got it, not even you. 2 years later Pops splits and before he goes —

LINCOLN.
He slips me 10 fifties in a clean handkerchief: "Hide this somewheres good, dont go blowing it, dont tell no one you got it, especially that Booth."

BOOTH.
Theyd been scheming together all along. They left separately but they was in agreement. Maybe they arrived at the same place at the same time, maybe they renewed they wedding vows, maybe they got another family.

LINCOLN.
Maybe they got 2 new kids. 2 boys. Different than us, though. Better.

BOOTH.
Maybe.

(Their glasses are empty. The whiskey bottle is empty too. Booth takes the champagne bottle from the ice tub. He pops the cork and pours drinks for his brother and himself.)

BOOTH.
I didnt mind them leaving cause you was there. Thats why Im hooked on us working together. If we could work together it would be like old times. They split and we got that room downtown. You was done with school and I stopped going. And we had to run around doing odd jobs just to keep the lights on and the heat going and thuh child protection bitch off our backs. It was you and me against thuh world, Link. It could be like that again.

LINCOLN.
BOOTH.
LINCOLN.
BOOTH.

LINCOLN.
Throwing thuh cards aint as easy as it looks.

BOOTH.
I aint stupid.

LINCOLN.
When you hung with us back then, you was just on thuh sidelines. Thuh perspective from thuh sidelines is thuh perspective of a customer. There was all kinds of things you didnt know nothing about.

BOOTH.
Lonny would entice folks into thuh game as they walked by. Thuh 2 folks on either side of ya looked like they was playing but they was only pretending tuh play. Just tuh generate excitement. You was moving thuh cards as fast as you could hoping that yr hands would be faster than yr customers eyes. Sometimes you won some-

times you lost what else is there to know?

LINCOLN.
Thuh customer is actually called the "Mark." You know why?

BOOTH.
Cause hes thuh one you got yr eye on. You mark him with yr eye.

LINCOLN.
LINCOLN.

BOOTH.
Im right, right?

LINCOLN.
Lemmie show you a few moves. If you pick up these yll have a chance.

BOOTH.
Yr playing.

LINCOLN.
Get thuh cards and set it up.

BOOTH.
No shit.

LINCOLN.
Set it up set it up.

(In a flash, Booth clears away the romantic table setting by gathering it all up in the tablecloth and tossing it aside. As he does so he reveals the "table" underneath: the 2 stacked monte milk crates and the cardboard playing surface. Booth holds the deck of cards out to Lincoln who hesitates for a moment then grabs them, quickly choosing three and laying them out.)

LINCOLN.
Thuh deuce of spades is thuh card tuh watch.

BOOTH.
I work with thuh deuce of hearts. But spades is cool.

LINCOLN.
Theres thuh Dealer, thuh Stickman, thuh Sides, thuh Lookout
and thuh Mark. I'll be thuh Dealer.

BOOTH.
I'll be thuh Lookout. Lemmie be thuh Lookout, right? I'll keep an
eye out for thuh cops. I got my piece in my pants.

LINCOLN.
You got it on you right now?

BOOTH.
I always carry it.

LINCOLN.
Even on a date? In yr own home?

BOOTH.
You never know, man.
(Rest)
So Im thuh Lookout.

LINCOLN.
Gimmie yr piece.

*(Booth gives Lincoln his gun. Lincoln moves the little wooden chair to
face right in front of the setup. He then puts the gun on the chair.)*

LINCOLN.
We dont need nobody standing on the corner watching for cops
cause there aint none. Thatll be the lookout.

BOOTH.
I'll be thuh Stickman, then.

LINCOLN.
Stickman knows the game inside out. You aint there yet. But you will be. You wanna learn good, be my Sideman. Playing along with the Dealer, moving the Mark to lay his money down. You wanna learn, right?

BOOTH.
I'll be thuh Side.

LINCOLN
Good.
(Rest)
First thing you learn is what is. Next thing you learn is what aint. You dont know what is you dont know what aint, you dont know shit.

BOOTH.
Right.

LINCOLN.
BOOTH.

BOOTH.
Whatchu looking at?

LINCOLN.
Im sizing you up.

BOOTH.
Oh yeah?!

LINCOLN.
Dealer always sizes up thuh crowd.

BOOTH.
Im yr Side, Link, Im on yr team, you dont go sizing up yr own team. You save looks like that for yr Mark.

LINCOLN.
Dealer always sizes up thuh crowd. Everybody out there is part of the crowd. His crew is part of the crowd, he himself is part of the crowd. Dealer always sizes up thuh crowd.

(Lincoln looks Booth over some more then looks around at an imaginary crowd.)

BOOTH.
Then what then what?

LINCOLN.
Dealer dont wanna play.

BOOTH.
Bullshit man! Come on you promised!

LINCOLN.
Thats thuh Dealers attitude. He *acts* like he dont wanna play. He holds back and thuh crowd, with their eagerness to see his skill and their willingness to take a chance, and their greediness to win his cash, the larceny in their hearts, all goad him on and push him to throw his cards, although of course the Dealer has been wanting to throw his cards all along. Only he dont never show it.

BOOTH.
Thats some sneaky shit, Link.

LINCOLN.
It sets thuh mood. You wanna have them in yr hand before you deal a hand, K?

BOOTH.
Cool. — K.

LINCOLN.
Right.

LINCOLN.
BOOTH.

BOOTH.
You sizing me up again?

LINCOLN.
Theres 2 parts to throwing thuh cards. Both parts are fairly com-
plicated. Thuh moves and thuh grooves, thuh talk and thuh walk,
thuh patter and thuh pitter pat, thuh rap and thuh flap: what yr
doing with yr mouth and what yr doing with yr hands.

BOOTH.
I got thuh words down pretty good.

LINCOLN.
You need to work on both.

BOOTH.
K.

LINCOLN.
A goodlooking walk and a dynamite talk captivates their entire
attention. The Mark focuses with 2 organs primarily: his eyes and
his ears. Leave one out you lose yr shirt. Captivate both, yr golden.

BOOTH.
So them times I seen you lose, them times I seen thuh Mark best
you, that was a time when yr hands werent fast enough or yr patter
werent right.

LINCOLN.
You could say that.

BOOTH.
So, there was plenty of times —

(Lincoln moves the cards around.)

79

LINCOLN.
You see what Im doing? Dont look at my hands, man, look at my eyes. Know what is and know what aint.

BOOTH.
What is?

LINCOLN.
My eyes.

BOOTH.
What aint?

LINCOLN.
My hands. Look at my eyes not my hands. And you standing there thinking how thuh fuck I gonna learn how tuh throw thuh cards if I be looking in his eyes? Look into my eyes and get yr focus. Dont think about learning how tuh throw thuh cards. Dont think about nothing. Just look into my eyes. Get yr focus.

BOOTH.
Theyre red.

LINCOLN.
Look into my eyes.

BOOTH.
You been crying?

LINCOLN.
Just look into my eyes, fool. Now. Look down at thuh cards. I been moving and moving and moving them around. Ready?

BOOTH.
Yeah.

LINCOLN.
Ok, Sideman, thuh Marks got his eye on you. Yr gonna show him

its easy.

BOOTH.
K.

LINCOLN.
Pick out thuh deuce of spades. Dont pick it up just point to it.

BOOTH.
This one, right?

LINCOLN.
Dont ask thuh Dealer if yr right, man, point to yr card with
confidence.

(Booth points.)

BOOTH.
That one.
(Rest)
Flip it over, man.

*(Lincoln flips over the card. It is in fact the deuce of spades. Booth
struts around gloating like a rooster. Lincoln is mildly crestfallen.)*

BOOTH.
Am I right or am I right?! Make room for 3-Card! Here comes
thuh champ!

LINCOLN.
Cool. Stay focused. Now we gonna add the second element. Listen.

(Lincoln moves the cards and speaks in a low hypnotic voice.)

LINCOLN.
Lean in close and watch me now: who see thuh black card who see
thuh black card I see thuh black card black cards thuh winner pick
thuh black card thats thuh winner pick thuh red card thats thuh

loser pick thuh other red card thats thuh other loser pick thuh black card you pick thuh winner. Watch me as I throw thuh cards. Here we go.

(Rest)

Who see thuh black card who see thuh black card? You pick thuh red card you pick a loser you pick thuh other red card you pick a loser you pick thuh black card thuh deuce of spades you pick a winner who sees thuh deuce of spades thuh one who sees it never fades watch me now as I throw thuh cards. Red losers black winner follow thuh deuce of spades chase thuh black deuce. Dark deuce will get you thuh win. One good pickll get you in 2 good picks you gone win. 10 will get you 20, 20 will get you 40.

(Rest)

Ima show you thuh cards: 2 red cards but only one spade. Dark winner in thuh center and thuh red losers on thuh sides. Pick uh red card you got a loser pick thuh other red card you got a loser pick thuh black card you got a winner. Watch me watch me watch me now.

(Rest)

Ok, 3-Card, you know which cards thuh deuce of spades?

BOOTH.
Yeah.

LINCOLN.
You sure? Yeah? You sure you sure or you just think you sure? Oh you sure you sure huh? Was you watching Links lighting fast express? Was you watching Link cause he the best? So you sure, huh? Point it out. Now, place yr bet and Linkll turn over yr card.

BOOTH.
What should I bet?

LINCOLN.
Dont bet nothing man, we just playing. Slap me 5 and point out thuh deuce.

(Booth slaps Lincoln 5, then points out a card which Lincoln flips over. It is in fact again the deuce of spades.)

BOOTH.
Yeah, baby! 3-Card got thuh moves! You didnt know lil bro had thuh stuff, huh? Think again, Link, think again.

LINCOLN.
You wanna learn or you wanna run yr mouth?

BOOTH.
Thought you had fast hands. Wassup? What happened tuh "Links Lightning Fast Express"? Looks like uh local train tuh me.

LINCOLN.
Thats yr whole motherfucking problem. Yr so busy running yr mouth you aint never gonna learn nothing! You think you something but you aint shit.

BOOTH.
I aint shit, I am *The* Shit. Shit. Wheres thuh dark deuce? Right there! Yes, baby!

LINCOLN.
Ok, 3-Card. Cool. Lets switch. Take thuh cards and show me whatcha got. Go on. Dont touch thuh cards too heavy just — its a light touch. Like yr touching Graces skin. Or, whatever, man, just a light touch. Like uh whisper.

BOOTH.
Like uh whisper.

(Booth moves the cards around, in an awkward imitation of his brother.)

LINCOLN.
Good.

BOOTH.
Yeah. All right. Look into my eyes.

(Booths speech is loud and his movements are jerky. He is doing worse

83

than when he threw the cards at the top of the play.)

BOOTH.
Watch-me-close-watch-me-close-now: who-see-thuh-black-card-
who-see-thuh-black-card? I-see-thuh-black-card. Here-it-is.
Thuh-black-card-is-thuh-winner. Pick-thuh-black-card-and-you-
pick-uh-winner. Pick-uh-red-card-and-you-pick-uh-loser. Theres-
thuh-loser-yeah-theres-thuh-red-card, theres-thuh-other-loser-
and-theres-thuh-black-card, thuh-winner. Watch-me-close-watch-
me-close-now: 3-Card-throws-thuh-cards-lightning-fast. 3-Card-
thats-me-and-Ima-last. Watch-me-throw-cause-here-I-go. See
thuh black card? Yeah? Who see I see you see thuh black card?

LINCOLN.
Hahahahhahahahahahahah!

*(Lincoln doubles over laughing. Booth puts on his coat and pockets
his gun.)*

BOOTH.
What?

LINCOLN.
Nothing, man, nothing.

BOOTH.
What?!

LINCOLN.
Yr just, yr just a little wild with it. You talk like that on thuh street
cards or no cards and theyll lock you up, man. Shit. Reminds me
of that time when you hung with us and we let you try being thuh
Stick cause you wanted it so bad. Thuh hustle was so simple.
Remember? I told you that when I put my hand in my left pocket you was to get thuh Mark tuh pick thuh card on that side. You
got to thinking something like Links left means my left some
dyslexic shit and turned thuh wrong card. There was 800 bucks on
the line and you fucked it up.

(Rest)
But it was cool, little bro, cause we made the money back.
It worked out cool.
(Rest)
So, yeah, I said a light touch, little bro. Throw thuh cards light.
Like uh whisper.

BOOTH.
Like Graces skin.

LINCOLN.
Like Graces skin.

BOOTH.
What time is it?

(Lincoln holds up his watch. Booth takes a look.)

BOOTH.
Bitch. *Bitch!* She said she was gonna show up around 8. 8-a-fucking-clock.

LINCOLN.
Maybe she meant 8 *a.m.*

BOOTH.
Yeah. She gonna come all up in my place talking bout how she *love* me. How she cant stop *thinking* bout me. Nother mans shit up in her nother mans thing in her nother mans dick on her breath.

LINCOLN.
Maybe something happened to her.

BOOTH.
Something happened to her all right. She trying to make a chump outa me. I aint her chump. I aint nobodys chump.

LINCOLN.
Sit. I'll go to the payphone on the corner. I'll —

BOOTH.
Thuh world puts its foot in yr face and you dont move. You tell thuh world tuh keep on stepping. But Im my own man, Link. I aint you.

(Booth goes out, slamming the door behind him.)

LINCOLN.
You got that right.

(After a moment Lincoln picks up the cards. He moves them around fast, faster, faster.)

Scene Six

Thursday night. The room looks empty, as if neither brother is home. Lincoln comes in. Hes high on liquor. He strides in, leaving the door slightly ajar.

LINCOLN.
Taaadaaaa!
(Rest)
(Rest)
Taadaa, motherfucker. Taadaa!
(Rest)
Booth — uh, 3-Card — you here? Nope. Good. Just as well. Ha Ha *Ha Ha Ha!*

(He pulls an enormous wad of money from his pocket. He counts it, slowly and luxuriously, arranging and smoothing the bills and sounding the amounts under his breath. He neatly rolls up the money, secures it with a rubber band and puts it back in his pocket. He relaxes in his

chair. Then he takes the money out again, counting it all over again, but this time quickly, with the touch of an expert hustler.)

LINCOLN.
You didnt go back, Link, you got back, you got it back you got yr shit back in thuh saddle, man, you got back in business. Walking in Luckys and you seen how they was looking at you? Lucky starts pouring for you when you walk in. And the women. You see how they was looking at you? Bought drinks for everybody. Bought drinks for Lucky. Bought drinks for Luckys damn dog. Shit. And thuh women be hanging on me and purring. And I be feeling that old call of thuh wild calling. I got more phone numbers in my pockets between thuh time I walked out that door and thuh time I walked back in than I got in my whole life. Cause my shit is *back*. And back better than it was when it left too. Shoot. Who thuh man? Link. Thats right. Purrrrring all up on me and letting me touch them and promise them shit. 3 of them sweethearts in thuh restroom on my dick all at once and I was *there* my shit was there. And Cookie just went out of my mind which is cool which is very cool. 3 of them. Fighting over it. Shit. Cause they knew I'd been throwing thuh cards. Theyd seen me on thuh corner with thuh old crew or if they aint seed me with they own eyes theyd heard word. Links thuh stink! Theyd heard word and they seed uh sad face on some poor sucker or a tear in thuh eye of some stupid fucking tourist and they figured it was me whod just took thuh suckers last dime, it was me who had all thuh suckers loot. They knew. They knew.

(Booth appears in the room. He was standing behind the screen, unseen all this time. He goes to the door, soundlessly, just stands there.)

LINCOLN.
And they was all in Luckys. Shit. And they was waiting for me to come in from my last throw. Cant take too many fools in one day, its bad luck, Link, so they was all waiting in there for me to come in thuh door and let thuh liquor start flowing and thuh music start going and let thuh boys who dont have thuh balls to get nothing but a regular job and uh weekly paycheck, let them crowd around and get in somehow on thuh excitement, and make way for thuh

ladies, so they can run they hands on my clothes and feel thuh
magic and imagine thuh man, with plenty to go around, living
and breathing underneath.
(Rest)
They all thought I was down and out! They all thought I was some
NoCount HasBeen LostCause motherfucker. But I got my shit
back. Thats right. They stepped on me and kept right on stepping.
Not no more. Who thuh man?! Goddamnit, who thuh —

(Booth closes the door.)

LINCOLN.
BOOTH.

(Rest)

LINCOLN.
Another evening to remember, huh?

BOOTH.
(Rest)
Uh — yeah, man, yeah. Thats right, thats right.

LINCOLN.
Had me a memorable evening myself.

BOOTH.
I got news.
(Rest)
What you been up to?

LINCOLN.
Yr news first.

BOOTH.
Its good.

LINCOLN.
Yeah?

BOOTH.
Yeah.

LINCOLN.
Go head then.

BOOTH.
(Rest)
Grace got down on her knees. Down on her knees, man. Asked *me*
tuh marry *her*.

LINCOLN.
Shit.

BOOTII.
Amazing Grace!

LINCOLN.
Lucky you, man.

BOOTH.
And guess where she was, I mean, while I was here waiting for her.
She was over at her house watching tv. I'd told her come over
Thursday and I got it all wrong and was thinking I said
Wednesday and here I was sitting waiting my ass off and all she
was doing was over at her house just watching tv.

LINCOLN.
Howboutthat.

BOOTH.
She wants to get married right away. Shes tired of waiting. Feels her
clock ticking and shit. Wants to have my baby. But dont look so
glum man, we gonna have a boy and we gonna name it after you.

LINCOLN.
Thats great, man. Thats really great.

BOOTH.
LINCOLN.

BOOTH.
Whats yr news?

LINCOLN.
(Rest)
Nothing.

BOOTH.
Mines good news, huh?

LINCOLN.
Yeah. Real good news, bro.

BOOTH.
Bad news is — well, shes real set on us living together. And she
always did like this place.
(Rest)
Yr gonna have to leave. Sorry.

LINCOLN.
No sweat.

BOOTH.
This was only a temporary situation anyhow.

LINCOLN.
No sweat man. You got a new life opening up for you, no sweat.
Graces moving in today? I can leave right now.

BOOTH.
I dont mean to put you out.

LINCOLN.
No sweat. I'll just pack up.

(Lincoln rummages around finding a suitcase and begins to pack his things.)

BOOTH.
Just like that, huh? "No sweat"?! Yesterday you lost yr damn job. You dont got no cash. You dont got no friends, no nothing, but you clearing out just like that and its "no sweat"?!

LINCOLN.
Youve been real generous and you and Grace need me gone and its time I found my own place.

BOOTH.
No sweat.

LINCOLN.
No sweat.
(Rest)
K. I'll spill it. I got another job, so getting my own place aint gonna be so bad.

BOOTH.
You got a new job! Doing what?

LINCOLN.
Security guard.

BOOTH.
(Rest)
Security guard. Howaboutthat.

(Lincoln continues packing the few things he has. He picks up a whiskey bottle.)

BOOTH.
Go head, take thuh med-sin, bro. You gonna need it more than me. I got, you know, I got my love to keep me warm and shit.

LINCOLN.
You gonna have to get some kind of work, or are you gonna let Grace support you?

BOOTH.
I got plans.

LINCOLN.
She might want you now but she wont want you for long if you dont get some kind of job. Shes a smart chick. And she cares about you. But she aint gonna let you treat her like some pack mule while shes out working her ass off and yr laying up in here scheming and dreaming to cover up thuh fact that you dont got no skills.

BOOTH.
Grace is very cool with who I am and where Im at, thank you.

LINCOLN.
It was just some advice. But, hey, yr doing great just like yr doing.

LINCOLN.
BOOTH.
LINCOLN.
BOOTH.

BOOTH.
When Pops left he didnt take nothing with him. I always thought that was fucked-up.

LINCOLN.
He was a drunk. Everything he did was always half regular and half fucked-up.

BOOTH.
Whyd he leave his clothes though? Even drunks gotta wear clothes.

LINCOLN.
Whyd he leave his clothes whyd he leave us? He was uh drunk,
bro. He — whatever, right? I mean, you aint gonna figure it out
by thinking about it. Just call it one of thuh great unsolved mys-
teries of existence.

BOOTH.
Moms had a man on thuh side.

LINCOLN.
Yeah? Pops had side shit going on too. More than one.
He would take me with him when he went to visit them. Yeah.
(Rest)
Sometimes he'd let me meet the ladies. They was all very nice. Very
polite. Most of them real pretty. Sometimes he'd let me watch. Most
of thuh time I was just outside on thuh porch or in thuh lobby or
in thuh car waiting for him but sometimes he'd let me watch.

BOOTH.
What was it like?

LINCOLN.
Nothing. It wasnt like nothing. He made it seem like it was this
big deal this great thing he was letting me witness but it wasnt
like nothing.
(Rest)
One of his ladies liked me, so I would do her after he'd done her.
On thuh sly though. He'd be laying there, spent and sleeping and
snoring and her and me would be sneaking it.

BOOTH.
Shit.

LINCOLN.
It was alright.

93

BOOTH.
LINCOLN.

(Lincoln takes his crumpled Abe Lincoln getup from the closet. Isnt sure what to do with it.)

BOOTH.
Im gonna miss you — coming home in that getup. I dont even got a picture of you in it for the album.

LINCOLN.
(Rest)
Hell, I'll put it on. Get thuh camera get thuh camera.

BOOTH.
Yeah?

LINCOLN.
What thuh fuck, right?

BOOTH.
Yeah, what thuh fuck.

(Booth scrambles around the apartment and finds the camera. Lincoln quickly puts on the getup, including 2 thin smears of white pancake makeup, more like war paint than whiteface.)

LINCOLN.
They didnt fire me cause I wasnt no good. They fired me cause they was cutting back. Me getting dismissed didnt have no reflection on my performance. And I was a damn good Honest Abe considering.

BOOTH.
Yeah. You look great man, really great. Fix yr hat. Get in thuh light. Smile.

LINCOLN.
Lincoln didnt never smile.

BOOTH.
Sure he smiled.

LINCOLN.
No he didnt, man, you seen thuh pictures of him. In all his pictures he was real serious.

BOOTH.
You got a new job, yr having a good day, right?

LINCOLN.
Yeah.

BOOTH.
So smile.

LINCOLN.
Snapshots gonna look pretty stupid with me —

(Booth takes a picture.)

BOOTH.
Thisll look great in thuh album.

LINCOLN.
Lets take one together, you and me.

BOOTH.
No thanks. Save the film for the wedding.

LINCOLN.
This wasnt a bad job. I just outgrew it. I could put in a word for you down there, maybe when business picks up again theyd hire you.

BOOTH.
No thanks. That shit aint for me. I aint into pretending Im someone else all day.

LINCOLN.
I was just sitting there in thuh getup. I wasnt pretending nothing.

BOOTH.
What was going on in yr head?

LINCOLN.
I would make up songs and shit.

BOOTH.
And think about women.

LINCOLN.
Sometimes.

BOOTH.
Cookie.

LINCOLN.
Sometimes.

BOOTH.
And how she came over here one night looking for you.

LINCOLN.
I was at Luckys.

BOOTH.
She didnt know that.

LINCOLN.
I was drinking.

BOOTH.
All she knew was you couldnt get it up. You couldnt get it up with her so in her head you was tired of her and had gone out to screw somebody new and this time maybe werent never coming back.
(Rest)

She had me pour her a drink or 2. I didnt want to. She wanted to get back at you by having some fun of her own and when I told her to go out and have it, she said she wanted to have her fun right here. With me.
[(Rest)
And then, just like that, she changed her mind.
(Rest)
But she'd hooked me. That bad part of me that I fight down every-day. You beat yrs down and it stays there dead but mine keeps coming up for another round. And the bad part of me took her clothing off and carried her into thuh bed and had her, Link, yr Cookie. It wasnt just thuh bad part of me it was all of me, man, I had her. Yr damn wife. Right in that bed.]

LINCOLN.
I used to think about her all thuh time but I dont think about her no more.

BOOTH.
I told her if she dumped you I'd marry her but I changed my mind.

LINCOLN.
I dont think about her no more.

BOOTH.
You dont go back.

LINCOLN.
Nope.

BOOTH.
Cause you cant. No matter what you do you cant get back to being who you was. Best you can do is just pretend to be yr old self.

LINCOLN.
Yr outa yr mind.

BOOTH.
Least Im still me!

LINCOLN.
Least I work. You never did like to work. You better come up with
some kinda way to bring home the bacon or Gracell drop you like
a hot rock.

BOOTH.
I got plans!

LINCOLN.
Yeah, you gonna throw thuh cards, right?

BOOTH.
Thats right!

LINCOLN.
You a double left-handed motherfucker who dont stand a chance
in all get out out there throwing no cards.

BOOTH.
You scared. You scared I got yr shit.

LINCOLN.
You aint never gonna do nothing.

BOOTH.
You scared you gonna throw and Ima kick yr ass — like yr boss
kicked yr ass like yr wife kicked yr ass — then Ima go out there
and do thuh cards like you do and Ima be thuh man and you aint
gonna be shit.
(Rest)
Ima set it up. And you gonna throw. Or are you scared?

LINCOLN.
Im gone.

(Lincoln goes to leave.)

BOOTH.
Fuck that!

LINCOLN.
BOOTH.

LINCOLN.
Damn. I didnt know it went so deep for you lil bro. Set up the cards.

BOOTH.
Thought you was gone.

LINCOLN.
Set it up.

BOOTH.
Ima kick yr ass.

LINCOLN.
Set it up!

(Booth hurriedly sets up the milk crates and cardboard top. Lincoln throws the cards.)

LINCOLN.
Lean in close and watch me now: who see thuh black card who see thuh black card I see thuh black card black cards thuh winner pick thuh black card thats thuh winner pick thuh red card thats thuh loser pick thuh other red card thats thuh other loser pick thuh black card you pick thuh winner. Who see thuh black card who see thuh black card? You pick thuh red card you pick a loser you pick that red card you pick a loser you pick thuh black card thuh deuce of spades you pick a winner who sees thuh deuce of spades thuh one who sees it never fades watch me now as I throw thuh cards. Red losers black winner follow thuh deuce of spades chase thuh black deuce. Dark deuce will get you thuh win. 10 will get you 20,

20 will get you 40. One good pickll get you in 2 good picks and you gone win.
(Rest)
Ok, man, wheres thuh black deuce?

(Booth points to a card. Lincoln flips it over. It is the deuce of spades.)

BOOTH.
Who thuh man?!

(Lincoln turns over the other 2 cards, looking at them confusedly.)

LINCOLN.
Hhhhh.

BOOTH.
Who thuh man, Link?! Huh? Who thuh man, Link?!?!

LINCOLN.
You thuh man, man.

BOOTH.
I got yr shit down.

LINCOLN.
Right.

BOOTH.
"Right"? All you saying is "right"?
(Rest)
You was out on the street throwing. Just today. Werent you? You wasnt gonna tell me.

LINCOLN.
Tell you what?

BOOTH.
That you was out throwing.

LINCOLN.
I was gonna tell you, sure. Cant go and leave my little bro out thuh loop, can I? Didnt say nothing cause I thought you heard. Did all right today but Im still rusty, I guess. But hey — yr getting good.

BOOTH.
But I'll get out there on thuh street and still fuck up, wont I?

LINCOLN.
You seem pretty good, bro.

BOOTH.
You gotta do it for real, man.

LINCOLN.
I am doing it for real. And yr getting good.

BOOTH.
I dunno. It didnt feel real. Kinda felt — well it didnt feel real.

LINCOLN.
We're missing the essential elements. The crowd, the street, thuh traffic sounds, all that.

BOOTH.
We missing something else too, thuh thing thatll really make it real.

LINCOLN.
Whassat, bro?

BOOTH.
Thuh cash. Its just bullshit without thuh money. Put some money down on thuh table then itd be real, then youd do it for real, then I'd win it for real.
(Rest)
And dont be looking all glum like that. I know you got money. A whole pocketful. Put it down.

LINCOLN.
BOOTH.

BOOTH.
You scared of losing it to thuh man, chump? Put it down, less you
think thuh kid who got two left hands is gonna give you uh left
hook. Put it down, bro, put it down.

(Lincoln takes the roll of bills from his pocket and places it on the table.)

BOOTH.
How much you got there?

LINCOLN.
500 bucks.

BOOTH.
Cool.
(Rest)
Ready?

LINCOLN.
Does it feel real?

BOOTH.
Yeah. Clean slate. Take it from the top. "One good pickll get you in
2 good picks and you gone win."
(Rest)
Go head.

LINCOLN.
Watch me now:

BOOTH.
Woah, man, woah.
(Rest)
You think Ima chump.

LINCOLN.
No I dont.

BOOTH.
You aint going full out.

LINCOLN.
I was just getting started.

BOOTH.
But when you got good and started you wasnt gonna go full out.
You wasnt gonna go all out. You was gonna do thuh pussy shit, not
thuh real shit.

LINCOLN.
I put my money down. Money makes it real.

BOOTH.
But not if I dont put no money down tuh match it.

LINCOLN.
You dont got no money.

BOOTH.
I got money!

LINCOLN.
You aint worked in years. You dont got shit.

BOOTH.
I got money.

LINCOLN.
Whatcha been doing, skimming off my weekly paycheck and
squirreling it away?

BOOTH.
I got money.

(Rest)
(They stand there sizing eachother up. Booth breaks away, going over to his hiding place from which he gets an old nylon stocking with money in the toe, a knot holding the money secure.)

LINCOLN.
BOOTH.

BOOTH.
You know she was putting her stuff in plastic bags? She was just putting her stuff in plastic bags not putting but shoving. She was shoving her stuff in plastic bags and I was standing in thuh door-way watching her and she was so busy shoving thuh shit she didnt see me. "I aint made of money," thats what he always saying. The guy she had on the side. I would catch them together sometimes. Thuh first time I cut school I got tired of hanging out so I goes home — figured I could tell Mom I was sick and cover my ass. Come in thuh house real slow cause Im sick and moving slow and quiet. He had her bent over. They both had all they clothes on like they was about to do something like go out dancing cause they was dressed to thuh 9s but at thuh last minute his pants had fallen down and her dress had flown up and theyd ended up doing some-thing else.
(Rest)
They didnt see me come in, they didnt see me watching them, they didnt see me going out. That was uh Thursday. Something told me tuh cut school thuh next Thursday and sure enough — . He was her Thursday man. Every Thursday. Yeah. And Thursday nights she was always all cleaned up and fresh and smelling nice. Serving up dinner. And Pops would grab her cause she was all bright and she would look at me, like she didnt know that I knew but she was ask-ing me not to tell nohow. She was asking me to — oh who knows.
(Rest)
She was talking with him one day, her sideman, her Thursday dude, her backdoor man, she needed some money for something, thered been some kind of problem some kind of mistake had been made some kind of mistake that needed cleaning up and she was asking Mr. Thursday for some money to take care of it. "I aint

made of money," he says. He was putting his foot down. And then there she was 2 months later not showing yet, maybe she'd got rid of it maybe she hadnt maybe she'd stuffed it along with all her other things in them plastic bags while he waited outside in thuh car with thuh motor running. She musta known I was gonna walk in on her this time cause she had my payoff — my *inheritance* — she had it all ready for me. 500 dollars in a nylon stocking. Huh.

(He places the stuffed nylon stocking on the table across from Lincolns money roll.)

BOOTH.
Now its real.

LINCOLN.
Dont put that down.

BOOTH.
Throw thuh cards.

LINCOLN.
I dont want to play.

BOOTH.
Throw thuh fucking cards, man!!

LINCOLN.
(Rest)
2 red cards but only one black. Pick thuh black you pick thuh winner. All thuh cards are face down you point out thuh cards and then you move them around. Now watch me now, now watch me real close. Put thuh winning deuce down in the center put thuh loser reds on either side then you just move thuh cards around. Move them slow or move them fast, Links thuh king he gonna last.
(Rest)
Wheres thuh deuce of spades?

(Booth chooses a card and chooses correctly.)

105

BOOTH.
HA!

LINCOLN.
One good pickll get you in 2 good picks and you gone win.

BOOTH.
I know man I know.

LINCOLN.
Im just doing thuh talk.

BOOTH.
Throw thuh fucking cards!

(Lincoln throws the cards.)

LINCOLN.
Lean in close and watch me now: who see thuh black card who see
thuh black card I see thuh black card black cards thuh winner pick
thuh black card thats thuh winner pick thuh red card thats thuh
loser pick thuh other red card thats thuh other loser pick thuh
black card you pick thuh winner. Watch me as I throw thuh cards.
Here we go.
(Rest)
Ima show you thuh cards: 2 red cards but only one spade. Dark
winner in thuh center and thuh red losers on thuh sides. Pick uh
red card you got a loser pick thuh other red card you got a loser
pick thuh black card you got a winner. Watch me watch me watch
me now.
(Rest)
Who see thuh black card who see thuh black card? You pick thuh
red card you pick a loser you pick that red card you pick a loser
you pick thuh black card thuh deuce of spades you pick a winner
who sees thuh deuce of spades thuh one who sees it never fades
watch me now as I throw thuh cards. Red losers black winner follow thuh deuce of spades chase thuh black deuce. Dark deuce will
get you thuh win.

(Rest)
Ok, 3-Card, you know which cards thuh deuce of spades? This is
for real now, man. You pick wrong Im in yr wad and I keep mines.

BOOTH.
I pick right I got yr shit.

LINCOLN.
Yeah.

BOOTH.
Plus I beat you for real.

LINCOLN.
Yeah.
(Rest)
You think we're really brothers?

BOOTH.
Huh?

LINCOLN.
I know we *brothers,* but is we really brothers, you know, blood
brothers or not, you and me, whatduhyathink?

BOOTH.
I think we're brothers.

BOOTH.
LINCOLN.
BOOTH.
LINCOLN.
BOOTH.
LINCOLN.

LINCOLN.
Go head man, wheres thuh deuce?

(In a flash Booth points out a card.)

LINCOLN.
You sure?

BOOTH.
Im sure!

LINCOLN.
Yeah? Dont touch thuh cards, now.

BOOTH.
Im sure.

(The 2 brothers lock eyes. Lincoln turns over the card that Booth selected and Booth, in a desperate break of concentration, glances down to see that he has chosen the wrong card.)

LINCOLN.
Deuce of hearts, bro. Im sorry. Thuh deuce of spades was this one.
(Rest)
I guess all this is mines.

(He slides the money toward himself.)

LINCOLN.
You were almost right. Better luck next time.
(Rest)
Aint yr fault if yr eyes aint fast. And you cant help it if you got 2 left hands, right? Throwing cards aint thuh whole world. You got other shit going for you. You got Grace.

BOOTH.
Right.

LINCOLN.
Whassamatter?

BOOTH.
Mm.

LINCOLN.
Whatsup?

BOOTH.
Nothing.

LINCOLN
(Rest)
It takes a certain kind of understanding to be able to play this game.
(Rest)
I still got thuh moves, dont I?

BOOTH.
Yeah you still got thuh moves.

(Lincoln cant help himself. He chuckles.)

LINCOLN.
I aint laughing at you, bro, Im just laughing. Shit there is so much
to this game. This game is — there is just so much to it.

(Lincoln, still chuckling, flops down in the easy chair. He takes up the
nylon stocking and fiddles with the knot.)

LINCOLN.
Woah, she sure did tie this up tight, didnt she?

BOOTH.
Yeah. I aint opened it since she gived it to me.

LINCOLN.
Yr kidding. 500 dollars and you aint never opened it? Shit. Sure is
tied tight. She said heres 500 bucks and you didnt undo thuh knot
to get a look at the cash? You aint needed to take a peek in all these
years? Shit. I woulda opened it right away. Just a little peek.

BOOTH.
I been saving it.
(Rest)
Oh, dont open it, man.

LINCOLN.
How come?

BOOTH.
You won it man, you dont gotta go opening it.

LINCOLN.
We gotta see whats in it.

BOOTH.
We *know* whats in it. Dont open it.

LINCOLN.
You are a chump, bro. There could be millions in here! There could be nothing! I'll open it.

BOOTH.
Dont.

LINCOLN.
BOOTH.

(Rest)

LINCOLN.
Shit this knot aint coming out. I could cut it, but that would spoil the whole effect, wouldnt it? Shit. Sorry. I aint laughing at you Im just laughing. Theres so much about those cards. You think you can learn them just by watching and just by playing but there is more to them cards than that. And — . Tell me something, Mr. 3-Card, she handed you this stocking and she said there was money in it and then she split and you say you didnt open it. Howd you know she was for real?

BOOTH.
She was for real.

LINCOLN.
How you know?! She coulda been jiving you, bro. Jiving you that
there really *was* money in this thing. Jiving you big time. Its like
thuh cards. And ooooh you certainly was persistent. But you was
in such a hurry to learn thuh last move that you didnt bother
learning thuh first one. That was yr mistake. Cause its thuh first
move that separates thuh Player from thuh Played. And thuh first
move is to know that there aint no winning. Taadaaa! It may look
like you got a chance but the only time you pick right is when
thuh man lets you. And when its thuh real deal, when its thuh real
fucking deal, bro, and thuh moneys on thuh line, thats when thuh
man wont want you picking right. He will want you picking
wrong so he will make you pick wrong. Wrong wrong wrong.
Ooooh, you thought you was finally happening, didnt you? You
thought yr ship had come in or some shit, huh? Thought you was
uh Player. But I played you, bro.

BOOTH.
Fuck you. Fuck you FUCK YOU *FUCK YOU!!*

LINCOLN.
Whatever, man. Damn this knot is tough. Ima cut it.

*(Lincoln reaches in his boot, pulling out a knife. He chuckles all the
while.)*

LINCOLN.
Im not laughing at you, bro, Im just laughing.

*(Booth chuckles with him. Lincoln holds the knife high, ready to cut
the stocking.)*

LINCOLN.
Turn yr head. You may not wanna look.

111

(Booth turns away slightly. They both continue laughing. Lincoln brings the knife down to cut the stocking.)

BOOTH.
I popped her.

LINCOLN.
Huh?

BOOTH.
Grace. I popped her. Grace.
(Rest)
Who thuh fuck she think she is doing me like she done? Telling me I dont got nothing going on. I showed her what I got going on. Popped her good. Twice. 3 times. Whatever.
(Rest)
She aint dead.
(Rest)
She werent wearing my ring I gived her. Said it was too small. Fuck that. Said it hurt her. Fuck that. Said she was into bigger things. *Fuck* that. Shes alive not to worry, she aint going out that easy, shes alive shes shes —

LINCOLN.
Dead. Shes —

BOOTH.
Dead.

LINCOLN.
Ima give you back yr stocking, man. Here, bro —

BOOTH.
Only so long I can stand that little brother shit. Can only take it so long. Im telling you —

LINCOLN.
Take it back, man —

BOOTH.
That little bro shit had to go —

LINCOLN.
Cool —

BOOTH.
Like Booth went —

LINCOLN.
Here, 3-Card —

BOOTH.
That Booth shit is over. 3-Cards thuh man now —

LINCOLN.
Ima give you yr stocking back, 3-Card —

BOOTH.
Who thuh man now, huh? Who thuh man now?! Think you can
fuck with me, motherfucker think again motherfucker think
again! Think you can take me like Im just some chump some two
lefthanded pussy dickbreath chump who you can take and then go
laugh at. Aint laughing at me you was just laughing bunch uh
bullshit and you know it.

LINCOLN.
Here. Take it.

BOOTH.
I aint gonna be needing it. Go on. You won it you open it.

LINCOLN.
No thanks.

BOOTH.
Open it open it open it open it. *OPEN IT!!!*
(Rest)

Open it up, bro.

LINCOLN.
BOOTH.

(Lincoln brings the knife down to cut the stocking. In a flash, Booth grabs Lincoln from behind. He pulls his gun and thrusts it into the left side of Lincolns neck. They stop there poised.)

LINCOLN.
Dont.

(Booth shoots Lincoln. Lincoln slumps forward, falling out of his chair and onto the floor. He lies there dead. Booth paces back and forth, like a panther in a cage, holding his gun.)

BOOTH.
Think you can take my shit? My shit. That shit was mines. I kept it. Saved it. All this while. Through thick and through thin. Through fucking thick and through fucking thin, motherfucker. And you just gonna come up in here and mock my shit and call me two lefthanded talking bout how she coulda been jiving me then go steal from me? My *inheritance*. You stole my *inheritance*, man. That aint right. That aint right and you know it. You had yr own. And you blew it. You *blew it*, motherfucker! I saved mines and you blew yrs. Thinking you all that and blew yr shit. And I *saved* mines.
(Rest)
You aint gonna be needing yr fucking money-roll no more, dead motherfucker, so I will pocket it thank you.
(Rest)
Watch me close watch me close now: Ima go out there and make a name for myself that dont have nothing to do with you. And 3-Cards gonna be in everybodys head and in everybodys mouth like Link was.
(Rest)
Ima take back my inheritance too. It was mines anyhow. Even when you stole it from me it was still mines cause she gave it to me. She didnt give it to you. And I been saving it all this while.

(He bends to pick up the money-filled stocking. Then he just crumples. As he sits beside Lincolns body, the money-stocking falls away. Booth holds Lincolns body, hugging him close. He sobs.)

BOOTH.
AAAAAAAAAAAAAAAAAAAAH!

End of Play

PROPERTY LIST

Playing cards
Cardboard playing board
2 milk crates
Lincoln costume (frock coat, pants, beard, top hat, necktie,
    white pancake makeup)
Bottle of whiskey
Two glasses
Gun (BOOTH)
Cold cream (LINCOLN)
Photo album (BOOTH)
Chinese food in containers, cans of soda, fortune cookies
    (LINCOLN)
Guitar (LINCOLN)
2 pairs of shoes (BOOTH)
2 belts (BOOTH)
2 new suits with price tags (BOOTH)
2 neckties (BOOTH)
2 shirts (BOOTH)
Magazines (BOOTH)
Folding screen (BOOTH)
Money (LINCOLN)
Box of condoms (BOOTH)
Blanket (BOOTH)
Plastic cup (LINCOLN)
Champagne on ice (BOOTH)
Plates and silverware (BOOTH)
Food (BOOTH)
Tablecloth (BOOTH)
Candles (BOOTH)
2 matching silk dressing-gowns (BOOTH)
Watch (LINCOLN)
Suitcase (LINCOLN)
Camera (BOOTH)
Nylon stockings with money in the toe (BOOTH)
Knife (LINCOLN)
Wad of money (LINCOLN)

SOUND EFFECTS

Gunshot

NEW PLAYS

★ YELLOW FACE by David Henry Hwang. Asian-American playwright DHH leads a protest against the casting of Jonathan Pryce as the Eurasian pimp in the original Broadway production of *Miss Saigon*, condemning the practice as "yellowface." The lines between truth and fiction blur with hilarious and moving results in this unreliable memoir. "A pungent play of ideas with a big heart." —*Variety.* "Fabulously inventive." —*The New Yorker.* [5M, 2W] ISBN: 978-0-8222-2301-6

★ 33 VARIATIONS by Moisés Kaufmann. A mother coming to terms with her daughter. A composer coming to terms with his genius. And, even though they're separated by 200 years, these two people share an obsession that might, even just for a moment, make time stand still. "A compellingly original and thoroughly watchable play for today." —*Talkin' Broadway.* [4M, 4W] ISBN: 978-0-8222-2392-4

★ BOOM by Peter Sinn Nachtrieb. A grad student's online personal ad lures a mysterious journalism student to his subterranean research lab. But when a major catastrophic event strikes the planet, their date takes on evolutionary significance and the fate of humanity hangs in the balance. "Darkly funny dialogue." —*NY Times.* "Literate, coarse, thoughtful, sweet, scabrously inappropriate." —*Washington City Paper.* [1M, 2W] ISBN: 978-0-8222-2370-2

★ LOVE, LOSS AND WHAT I WORE by Nora Ephron and Delia Ephron, based on the book by Ilene Beckerman. A play of monologues and ensemble pieces about women, clothes and memory covering all the important subjects—mothers, prom dresses, mothers, buying bras, mothers, hating purses and why we only wear black. "Funny, compelling." —*NY Times.* "So funny and so powerful." —*WowOwow.com.* [5W] ISBN: 978-0-8222-2355-9

★ CIRCLE MIRROR TRANSFORMATION by Annie Baker. When four lost New Englanders enrolled in Marty's community center drama class experiment with harmless games, hearts are quietly torn apart, and tiny wars of epic proportions are waged and won. "Absorbing, unblinking and sharply funny." —*NY Times.* [2M, 3W] ISBN: 978-0-8222-2445-7

★ BROKE-OLOGY by Nathan Louis Jackson. The King family has weathered the hardships of life and survived with their love for each other intact. But when two brothers are called home to take care of their father, they find themselves strangely at odds. "Engaging dialogue." —*TheaterMania.com.* "Assured, bighearted." —*Time Out.* [3M, 1W] ISBN: 978-0-8222-2428-0

DRAMATISTS PLAY SERVICE, INC.
440 Park Avenue South, New York, NY 10016   212-683-8960   Fax 212-213-1539
postmaster@dramatists.com   www.dramatists.com

NEW PLAYS

★ **A CIVIL WAR CHRISTMAS: AN AMERICAN MUSICAL CELEBRA-TION by Paula Vogel, music by Daryl Waters.** It's 1864, and Washington, D.C. is settling down to the coldest Christmas Eve in years. Intertwining many lives, this musical shows us that the gladness of one's heart is the best gift of all. "Boldly inventive theater, warm and affecting." –*Talkin' Broadway.* "Crisp strokes of dialogue." –*NY Times.* [12M, 5W] ISBN: 978-0-8222-2361-0

★ **SPEECH & DEBATE by Stephen Karam.** Three teenage misfits in Salem, Oregon discover they are linked by a sex scandal that's rocked their town. "Savvy comedy." –*Variety.* "Hilarious, cliché-free, and immensely entertaining." –*NY Times.* "A strong, rangy play." –*NY Newsday.* [2M, 2W] ISBN: 978-0-8222-2286-6

★ **DIVIDING THE ESTATE by Horton Foote.** Matriarch Stella Gordon is determined not to divide her 100-year-old Texas estate, despite her family's declining wealth and the looming financial crisis. But her three children have another plan. "Goes for laughs and succeeds. –*NY Daily News.* "The theatrical equivalent of a page-turner." –*Bloomberg.com.* [4M, 9W] ISBN: 978-0-8222-2398-6

★ **WHY TORTURE IS WRONG, AND THE PEOPLE WHO LOVE THEM by Christopher Durang.** Christopher Durang turns political humor upside down with this raucous and provocative satire about America's growing homeland "insecurity." "A smashing new play." –*NY Observer.* "You may laugh yourself silly." –*Bloomberg News.* [4M, 3W] ISBN: 978-0-8222-2401-3

★ **FIFTY WORDS by Michael Weller.** While their nine-year-old son is away for the night on his first sleepover, Adam and Jan have an evening alone together, beginning a suspenseful nightlong roller-coaster ride of revelation, rancor, passion and humor. "Mr. Weller is a bold and productive dramatist." –*NY Times.* [1M, 1W] ISBN: 978-0-8222-2348-1

★ **BECKY'S NEW CAR by Steven Dietz.** Becky Foster is caught in middle age, middle management and in a middling marriage—with no prospects for change on the horizon. Then one night a socially inept and grief-struck millionaire stumbles into the car dealership where Becky works. "Gently and consistently funny." –*Variety.* "Perfect blend of hilarious comedy and substantial weight." –*Broadway Hour.* [4M, 3W] ISBN: 978-0-8222-2393-1

DRAMATISTS PLAY SERVICE, INC.
440 Park Avenue South, New York, NY 10016 212-683-8960 Fax 212-213-1539
postmaster@dramatists.com www.dramatists.com

NEW PLAYS

★ **AT HOME AT THE ZOO by Edward Albee.** Edward Albee delves deeper into his play THE ZOO STORY by adding a first act, HOMELIFE, which precedes Peter's fateful meeting with Jerry on a park bench in Central Park. "An essential and heartening experience." *–NY Times.* "Darkly comic and thrilling." *–Time Out.* "Genuinely fascinating." *–Journal News.* [2M, 1W] ISBN: 978-0-8222-2317-7

★ **PASSING STRANGE book and lyrics by Stew, music by Stew and Heidi Rodewald, created in collaboration with Annie Dorsen.** A daring musical about a young bohemian that takes you from black middle-class America to Amsterdam, Berlin and beyond on a journey towards personal and artistic authenticity. "Fresh, exuberant, bracingly inventive, bitingly funny, and full of heart." *–NY Times.* "The freshest musical in town!" *–Wall Street Journal.* "Excellent songs and a vulnerable heart." *–Variety.* [4M, 3W] ISBN: 978-0-8222-2400-6

★ **REASONS TO BE PRETTY by Neil LaBute.** Greg really, truly adores his girlfriend, Steph. Unfortunately, he also thinks she has a few physical imperfections, and when he mentions them, all hell breaks loose. "Tight, tense and emotionally true." *–Time Magazine.* "Lively and compulsively watchable." *–The Record.* [2M, 2W] ISBN: 978-0-8222-2394-8

★ **OPUS by Michael Hollinger.** With only a few days to rehearse a grueling Beethoven masterpiece, a world-class string quartet struggles to prepare their highest-profile performance ever—a televised ceremony at the White House. "Intimate, intense and profoundly moving." *–Time Out.* "Worthy of scores of bravissimos." *–BroadwayWorld.com.* [4M, 1W] ISBN: 978-0-8222-2363-4

★ **BECKY SHAW by Gina Gionfriddo.** When an evening calculated to bring happiness takes a dark turn, crisis and comedy ensue in this wickedly funny play that asks what we owe the people we love and the strangers who land on our doorstep. "As engrossing as it is ferociously funny." *–NY Times.* "Gionfriddo is some kind of genius." *–Variety.* [2M, 3W] ISBN: 978-0-8222-2402-0

★ **KICKING A DEAD HORSE by Sam Shepard.** Hobart Struther's horse has just dropped dead. In an eighty-minute monologue, he discusses what path brought him here in the first place, the fate of his marriage, his career, politics and eventually the nature of the universe. "Deeply instinctual and intuitive." *–NY Times.* "The brilliance is in the infinite reverberations Shepard extracts from his simple metaphor." *–TheaterMania.* [1M, 1W] ISBN: 978-0-8222-2336-8

DRAMATISTS PLAY SERVICE, INC.
440 Park Avenue South, New York, NY 10016 212-683-8960 Fax 212-213-1539
postmaster@dramatists.com www.dramatists.com